Burabau Quini
Recil,

Making Peace with My Past

Thank You, God's-
Blessings Always

Dr. Althea C Driver

Dr. Althea Driver

Author's Tranquility Press
ATLANTA, GEORGIA

Dr. Althea C Driver/Author's Tranquility Press
3900 N Commerce Dr. Suite 300 #1255
Atlanta, GA 30331, USA
www.authorstranquilitypress.com

Ordering Information:
Quantity sales. Special discounts are available on quantity purchases by corporations, associations, and others. For details, contact the "Special Sales Department" at the address above.

Making Peace with My Past/ Dr. Althea C Driver
Hardback: 978-1-964362-70-0
Paperback: 978-1-964362-05-2
eBook: 978-1-964362-06-9

CONTENTS

Foreword

"Making Peace with My Past" by Althea C. Moser Driver is a compelling journey of resilience, transformation, and self-discovery. The author reflects on a life marked by tumultuous experiences, addiction, and the challenges of homelessness, providing an intimate account of her struggles and triumphs.

The narrative unfolds with an acknowledgement that the past, no matter how chaotic, doesn't define the present or dictate the future. Althea Driver's candid storytelling reveals a profound shift in perspective, emphasizing the power of determination, positivity, and the belief in one's ability to lead a productive life.

The Author takes readers through the maze of complicated choices and mistakes that defined her earlier years. From the grip of addiction to moments of despair, the book candidly explores the author's journey, acknowledging the scars left by the past but emphasizing the importance of learning, growth, and the strength derived from overcoming adversity.

"Making Peace with My Past" serves as a beacon of hope and encouragement for those facing their own challenges. It underscores the significance of self-love, forgiveness, and the transformative journey toward healing. Althea's narrative inspires readers to embrace change, confront their past, and move forward with a renewed sense of purpose and gratitude.

In this memoir, Althea invites readers to witness her transformation from a life overshadowed by addiction and despair to a place of peace, gratitude, and self-empowerment. This story is a testament to the resilience of the human spirit and the possibilities that unfold when one decides to make peace with the past.

Raven Miller

Authors Tranquility Press

www.authorstranquilitypress.com

3900 N. Commerce Dr. Suite 300 #1255 Atlanta, GA 30344

Introduction

"WOW" What a life to have knowing that the past no longer affects the way I live. In fact, it has helped me become who I am knowing this has presented to me that I can have a productive life. I believe in me because I am determined to stay dynamic with a positive attitude that's full of energy, I don't know how many more years I have left but these are precious times for me, and I am grateful to be back. The past is the past. I will never go back no matter how the storms of life may rage you don't let it stop you if you know what I mean. Not being made to feel as though I have wasted life and now it is just too late for me to move forward in making something out of myself but to know that I can is a good thing. Today I know better because I have been taught a lesson well learned by the many experiences that I have gone through they were all signs and wonders of things to come some good and some not so good which is to be expected because this is what life teaches you the good, the bad, and the ugly.

My past was a part of me figuring out life and how to live it which led me to so many complicated choices and mistakes that I attempted to make, terrified me because I didn't know how to deal with what I was being confronted with. I knew I was headed for better things, leaving behind the past looking forward to becoming the person I was created to be. Because I know I have a lot to offer and a purpose for being here. I learned that God had a purpose for my life before I was even born. Be determined about what you desire to accomplish and pursue it such as the goals you want to achieve and go about fulfilling them. I have appreciated life this far even if my beginning was rough and seemed too complicated sometimes, I realized that each of us has courage that we don't realize we have. I've learned that courage is doing what you are afraid of doing. It's good to know when life throws you lemons make lemonade, not to mention the curve balls that come at you. I can't say that I'm no longer afraid of what life has to offer, but I feel that I am better prepared. I certainly deserve to be whole and at peace after everything I have been challenged with. Even when bad things happen, I must move on and focus on what I must do because yesterday was just that! Yesterday is gone forever, today is another day. For me Happiness is a choice, most importantly it's a gift one of many but to be unhappy is something you don't want to risk being a part of your life. Because it can and will create serious problems making life more difficult. Knowing that the past was left with scars and the memories of yesterday not only in my addiction but growing up as a young girl. Which led me down many wrong paths of not knowing what I should have known about life. It's hard to sometimes comprehend how things should have been prepared but wasn't and now that I am at the age of retirement and planning to enjoy life I am just getting involved in trying to accomplish what I should already have. a structured life enjoying what I have accomplished and worked for but none of that happened and yet I felt like a failure, too late to change what has happened in the past. There was a lot of learning I had yet to do and how awful it all seems to me now. But know this God has a specific plan for every one of our lives the quality of life is determine by the quality of your decisions which is what I've learned. One of the main keys to overcoming disappointment in life is learning to let go of the past by choosing to forgive those who have hurt or wronged you.

Don't let the regrets of yesterday destroy the hopes of tomorrow no matter what has happened, and I know it's not always the easiest thing to do. But you must move on, let go and release the past. Don't allow distractions are busyness of life get you off course ask yourself is this my purpose in life or am I wasting time being busy and not really making any progress. Keep your eyes on the prize that you are pursuing. Don't be distracted, don't spend time and energy on things that are not helping you fulfill your dreams and goals. Speak whatever it is you are seeking into existence and stand strong during troublesome times. When I first started getting deeper into my addiction. I had no idea what life for me would be like because of the habits I had consumed and endured for so long years to be exact.

Not realizing the danger and most importantly the damage, I was bringing upon myself, which caused a lot of hurt, pain and discomfort along the way. But thanks be to God that I still had a mind that I could think in a way to want change from that horrible way of living a life I would never want to experience again or see anyone else go through what I had gone through. You never know what you will be faced with as you go through life but know that when it's not the right way to live you can change the way you are living and start making positive moves in your life.

My life consisted of many afflictions and hardships that I did not see coming until it was too late. I had gotten caught up and would find myself indulging deeper into my addiction. My desire and intense longing to keep using and abusing my body for my satisfaction was causing me to develop anxiety and depression like never before. Not knowing the price, I would pay one day which almost cost me my life. I know how horrific being addicted to drugs and alcohol can become. It takes the best from you and puts you in a place that doesn't have anything to offer you except emotional trauma total darkness and death if you don't come to the fore front and realize the need to make change.

I can truly attest to this because I experienced and went through this pattern of life for years. I talked and dealt with those demonic spirits that once controlled my mind, my thoughts and the way I lived in very devastating and disastrous times. I wished there were times when I had never been born and then there were times when I wished I could change things and start all over again for the better, not seeing no way out of my circumstances. Oh yes and there were times when I wanted to give up, feeling like life had nothing to offer me and I would not make it or anything good would become of me. I knew I had to keep preserving by overcoming and eradicated mind you can be clear living in a confused and mixed-up world until I could see the hope, I had been waiting for shining through. In which case I went through years of suffering before I got to that doorway. I suffered tremendously my life was in shambles being torn apart because I was surrounded everyday with the desire of wanting drugs to keep me going no matter the cost or what I had to do to get them. The thought of me lowering my standard as a woman made no difference to me because it really didn't matter, I was on a mission to get what satisfied me.

Which was that high that you long for all the time. There is no end to it until you realize you are chasing a dream that will never be fulfilled. Just being truthful about my addiction and what it does to the human mind you have to come to the place of understanding that it must end regain your sanity and make the change that's necessary to have a productive life. I know there are many of you out there that can relate to me and where I am going with this.

Being real, this is what my life consisted of day in and day out for years. I dealt with the everyday struggles of trying to support and keep up with these destructive and demonic habits because I liked the feeling of high and I didn't want to stop neither was I trying to. Wishing I could stay high for the duration of my life. Today I feel like an absolute idiot for even having that mindset. You really don't know how we are affecting our mind and body when we pick up the self-inflicted habits of drugs, alcohol and cigarettes that can and will destroy your life if you don't seek to make the proper change.

I guess some of you would ask the question what is "*Proper Change*"? Change from doing what's wrong to doing what's right. That was something that took years for me to do because my thinking wasn't there and I wasn't thinking about the aftereffects of these deadly diseases, and I can assure you that it was not an overnight sensation or process. These habits take time and persistence and that depends totally on you. I went through a lot when I was going through my addiction stages which caused me to become homeless. Because of the choices I had made landed me in a world of chaos surrounded by people who were doing the exact same thing I had become, and addict addicted to drugs and alcohol. The people I met who had been living this way before it ever became a thought in my mind. Before I ever attempted to try using drugs, they were eager to share it with me until I got hooked and then I was on my own as far as supporting my habit.

I learned you will never have real friends in this world, only monsters you go for what you know, in other words you are in a dark and dangerous battle and it's all about survival, you have two choices in the matter you can choose to live or die. I really didn't realize what a big impact this was causing for me. Because I was struggling with my addiction and the many hardships that I was being faced with, not knowing what a normal life felt like or consisted of anymore. Being in that way for so long was not the easiest thing to stop doing, the more I did it the more it became a lethal weapon.

One that will take something so precious as your being and destroy who you are if you don't make up your mind to stop using and seek help for your addictions. Such is what I had accumulated in my life and was on my way to self-destruction enjoying the fleeting pleasures of drugs. I still remember some of those days when me and my friends would go to the place that we had discovered in the woods where we could have fun drinking and drugging as much as we wanted to. We didn't worry about the police because if they hadn't seen us, we didn't have to worry about them, they didn't go out of their way looking for drug addicts and homeless people.

Unless they needed to make there quoter for the month then they would come looking for us. They very seldom came into the woods, we called the weed patch, it was one of the many hangouts we had. It was next door to the convenient store called "Buddy's" After all those years Buddy's still exist. Unfortunately, the woods, those beautiful tall shade trees that once existed are no longer there, they have been replaced with condominiums. It was a place where we had access to food, beer, and wine. We could freely go and come as we pleased until some would get barred from the store because they would ask for money from customers, but if we didn't bother anyone, we could come in and get what we wanted. Because the place of residence was called the weed patch filled with tall shade trees prefect hangout for the summer. Not realizing the help, we all so desperately need. There were times after my life had become manageable, I would stop in at buddy's just to sit and reminisce of those days I shared with the people I once lived with. It was a place we would hang out because it was always something going on, there was lots of traffic in and out of those woods that we called the weed patch, but we were having our share of fun enjoying life not thinking about tomorrow or our own future.

We were living in our own world not knowing what tomorrow would bring or if we would live to see it. This went on for years, we breathed and lived that way in a world where we felt safe and secure to enjoy what we were used to doing. It was fun while it lasted, and we took advantage of it as the old saying goes good things must come to an end. And the day came when that all ended for change came and I made a conscious decision one that I knew I must do to have a better life and make sound decisions in which way I wanted to go.

The choice had presented itself and I had to believe and know within myself that this was the right thing to do considering what I had experienced and gone through. Leading up to everything I have learned that change can be exceptionally beneficial when we realize the need for it. Which is what I did although it wasn't the easiest thing to do, I am so glad that I had the strength and willingness to overcome. Making a positive move toward right thinking and right living wasn't easy to overcome the habits of addiction. But you never know what you can do until you make up your mind to do it.

We all have a wonderful creative mind that has been given to each of us, we must discover and use it in the right way because right thinking leads to right living and I have understood that once we recognize it, we will be able to do and live the life we have been given. I have learned to love me for who I am no matter my past and to know that to have a life we have got to want life because it is a precious gift to own therefore I cannot and will not waste any more of it. This I say to my sisters and brothers who are struggling with these addictive habits you do not have to stay there my best advice is to let it go and come to a place in life where you recognize and realize that we all need to seek help at some point and time. I am "Making Peace with My Past" changing course and moving to the next level of happiness.

I was centered around the right people who reached out and gave me the support and help that I needed. So, I say this to you if you don't believe that Jesus can help with your situation and change your life for the greater than seek help somewhere. Because today there are lots of ways and programs out there that offer help, please seek the help you need. It means a lot for me to be able to tell my story so that you will know that you are not alone in whatever it is you are dealing with that's trying to overshadow your life from moving forward and being productive.

Don't keep living in the shadows know for yourself that life can be better if you choose to do better. Change starts within make up your mind that this is what you are going to do by changing the way you live, think, and do things. We learn from the many mistakes that we all will make in this lifetime so let's get prepared to continue your journey to where it's going to take you. Are should I say where God is taken you. That sounds more like the right thing to say as I put this in the perspective that it will help enhance your lifestyle and standard of living.

I know from whence I have come there are many wonders ahead that await your undivided attention. It is so very important that once you have come through the storms and hardships of life to pay attention to where you are going. Because it's so easy to get distracted. Which is what happens when change begins to take place in our lives. This is what the enemy focuses on. He doesn't want to see the change that's coming and he's going to do everything he possibly can to stop you and there are many paths that he will take. Some of which we are very familiar with such as deception, depression, feelings of loneliness, discouragement, anxiety, nobody wants you and most of all unloved. I know this because I faced these very situations in the worst of times.

Despite what I was going through, believe me when I tell you this because it is so true. If you want help, He is there to see you through whatever trials and tribulations you are experiencing in your life. Right now, as I sit here writing about my life experience, I want you to believe in yourself and have the God kind of faith and confidence that it's going to take to see you through whatever comes your way.

Throughout my life I have been privileged to have the favor of God on my life when I didn't even know what the favor of God was.

I was going through and experiencing things that were too difficult to describe yet despite it all I am still here, there were many times I had brushes with death. Dealing with the trauma of a drug infested life that I was living. There was no easy fix for the mental and physical sufferings that I was dealing with as I faced the fires of affliction because of that lifestyle, the one in which I chose to live. I am thankful that I am here today to share with you the importances of one-way God shows his love is through mercy! As I share my story you will learn about the person who wrote this book in detail from how long I have been on this planet to how and what caused my life to change in the manner and way that it did.

This book is dedicated to those who are willing to forgive themselves, move forward and Make Peace with The Past in a healthy and wholesome way. With peace comes the promise of joy, a promise for the future. Moving on is the key to a healthy lifestyle. Which so many of us miss out on, if you stick to one thing and don't accept the change you will never make progress. The ability to bring people together is what makes people great. Making peace with the past and accepting the present, looking forward to a better and brighter future is so vital to life being authentic about yourself.

We all have a story and a past but remember the past is behind you, it can only hurt when you use it against yourself. It means moving on and removing the negative labels that's been placed on you. Forget the bad things that have happened in the past. Take them in stride and learn to view them as obstacles which helped me to grow from. Today marks a new beginning in life for me after everything I had been through the difficulties, bad times and hardships I later learned were all meant to strengthen me.

A lesson learned is always to be taken positively, we must understand that people go through much worse things which are beyond our imagination and still move on with life. The price of greatness is responsibility. I constantly remind myself of these very things' freedom is a feeling like no other powerful thing and with great power comes great responsibility. Many of us live in search of what life has to offer, not prepared for what the world has to offer.

Temptation and deception can be strong forces in our lives because we are no longer protected by our parents. Which is what happened to me. I did not fully understand freedom of choice and what to do with it or to know we should always strive to do good in every place that we can. I have embraced change and the gifts that have been implemented within me. I have learned to love and enjoy others, taken nothing for granted because every ounce of life is precious.

It's not to be sucked up in a vacuum never to be used. In the beginning of my story, I talk about the delusions and how it became so unmanageable because of my addiction to drugs and alcohol. Which led to homelessness and so many wrong turns along the way. Because once you start using it it's not going to stay recreational for the rest of your life, it doesn't work that way. As I struggled through those dark times, I felt isolated, alone, and most of all ashamed because of the way my life had turned out. However, through persistence and hard work I have seen how God takes our ugly circumstances and changes them into positive and beautiful things. He has done it for me, and I know He can and will do the same for you. If you want to change. Healing from the pain of abuse can be a struggle for so many because as people we suffer from self-rejection and the need to feel good about ourselves. This type of thought pattern can persist for years, and I tell myself about those silent years. Some of the hardest times for me involved feeling like there was no hope and nothing to look forward to because of the wasted years that had passed me by. Not knowing that we shape our dwelling and after words our dwelling shapes us. Habits take time to develop. We must unlearn some things since most of our habits didn't develop overnight. It's unrealistic to expect them to go away immediately.

There is no magic pill that will instantly undo the damage that has been there for many years. It requires the work of removal and replacement. The bible calls for taking off the old self putting on the new self. I am not exaggerating just telling the truth about what I am saying here. I am speaking from years of experience and many failed attempts at what I went through overcoming my addiction. The only way I could began the healing process of making peace with my past was the fact that I had to recognize that forgiveness was a key factor and that I needed help so that I could start the process of feeling confident in a positive way being honest with myself and others.

After years of being consumed with drugs, alcohol and living homeless you remember some of the things you went through you didn't think you would make it. And now when you look back over your life you see the reason those drugs and alcohol did not kill you, they brought me into full circles of myself a different outlook on life was happening in and around me. It's in these times we wonder what am I going to do now. And why has this happened, but we must know and understand that when we find ourselves in tumultuous situations, we all have a limited time here on earth how will you utilize your time. Life has many passing storms, and everyone experiences them in one way or another. If I knew the thing then that I know now I would not have gone that way.

Through the years, after overcoming my addictions I learned that strength is available to all who believe in themselves and confess their weaknesses and shortcomings. Sometime a troubled soul has only enough stamina left to admit, I can't do this alone and that's okay because in this mindset we surrender ourselves to God as we wait, we are in an acceptable position to watch him keep his promise. I will always be grateful for the place I come to occupy and take up space that I know is good space and most of all the beautiful message it sends. Today I am sharing the aftereffects of it all Making Peace with My Past a peace like no other. Despite everything, though it has been a very tough road I am grateful and most of all thankful to be here. Still standing I've learned that nothing is easy, nothing is free, if you want to be successful you must pay the price.

It is a good thing when you can learn to give the gift of yourself to help others and share words of encouragement because I know what life for me was like not knowing what to expect. But to know that the healing process had begun gave me hope to believe because I am making peace with my past, and I have no regrets. We all get lost in our thinking at some point and time in our lives. Before the change it took years for me to stop doing drugs and drinking because I liked what I was doing and had become addicted to the feeling and that makes it even harder to quiet. But to get to this place in life having a mind to want to change made all the difference.

It is also important to have realistic expectations for ourselves. If we accept only perfection, we are bound to be disappointed, and discouragement will set in. rather than give up, we must be determined knowing that I can and will overcome by taking our frustration and fears to another level of knowing this too shall pass. Once I found that peace my life started becoming more manageable. And the people that I met along the way helped me as I continued to do what I knew was best made all the differences in the world. Knowing that I would need help, I could not have done this on my own. It was no way possible we all need each other to survive the storms that come into our lives.

Bill Johnson once said, *"A storm you can sleep through is a storm that you have authority over."* Today the crippling path of resentment no longer exists. I am in a much better position, knowing that whatever you are going through you don't have to do it by yourself, there is help reach out ask and accept it. Your life is the story you will tell the world. Since I have come to the place of Making Peace with My Past I see now that everything happens in life for a reason and a purpose, and it was good that I was afflicted. Not that I'm proud to be speaking this way, but I came to the realization that had this not happened I would not be where I am today. It opened my eyes to the realization of what people need to know and understand about themselves even though He has given us power and dominion over our lives and the creation of the earth. He never makes a mistake, and His love never fails. I will do my best to summarize profound insight that the same God who rescued me from circumstances in the past is the same God who bless me, kept me and continually keep using me living confidently and fearlessly even when I fall because falling does not make me a failure staying there does. There are many unhappy endings on earth everything happens in your life is permeated for that purpose don't give up – grow up and always remember the true meaning of life.

As you and I live in this world we will never be perfect, not everybody knows this. Do not stress your mind out with the burden of trying to be something or someone you cannot be and that is perfect because it is impossible, and you will never get there just be yourself and believe in the one who created you because He is the *"Perfect One"* who will help you reach your goals and destiny.

Today I can move in a more profound way by sharing more about Making Peace with My Past. My life is a story of the many dangers I faced and yet through it all I survived because I wanted that change in me to start taking up residence. I want to share with you one of many things that's very important to each and every one that seeks to make change in life and that is to *"Never Give Up"* on self no matter what it seems like, looks like, or feels like or how difficult the journey is *"Never Give Up"* because there is hope through it all and you will experience that light at the end of the tunnel. Just keep believing in yourself and the one who created you and you will get there holding steadfast to your faith and beliefs.

I cannot begin to tell you how proud I am of myself for going the extra mile. My life tells my story because of what I went through and tell it in a way that you will understand how important it is to take care of yourself and make good and wise decisions. If my story is told I want to be the one to share it with the world not someone else because it's my place to share my experiences and what I went through. If I don't tell my story someone else will try and it want be told the way I know because nobody knows what life was like for me but me. There we time I was sick, cold, hungry without a place to stay and yet I survived that's why it's so important that we become who we are.

My story is special to me because it tells of what I went through and how much I overcame despite my failed attempts Because of His love for me. Regardless of what I had done during that time He did not leave me. His love is truly unconditional no matter where we are in life or what we are going through. In my first book I told you lots of things Jesus done for me during that time He showed me in many ways that He was and still is the greatest of all times very much alive. And very much in love with me and you which took me totally by surprise in so many ways you will feel and know His love.

I remember when he changed my life from being sick to healed from broke to bless when I should have been crazy, he kept me with a sane mind I am alive I survived, I was confused, and my life was totally out of control, but I would tell myself it will get better it made me stronger. You never know how good God is until He rescues you out of the storm like He did me. There were many miracles performed in my life before the transformation took place. After becoming born again my old life had changed and the new had begun because I had opened the door of my heart and invited Jesus to come in as Lord and Savior of my life. He opened my eyes to see the miracles that were performed when I did not love Him, he was there for me I will always remember those special moments.

This book about my past to the present was forged through time and trials. None of us come to love God deeply, to see Him clearly without first having and awakening to our interment depravity which can lead to a fuller whole life and an appreciation of God's love. We must always remember whose image we are created in and the quality of who made us. I'm not rewriting my story. I am here to tell you that what I have written is a true story about my life and the ups and downs of what I went through and where it has brought me today. I hope that in writing my life story it will impact the lives of others in a very profound and positive way to know and understand that we cannot make a life we have to live the life we have been given. It's especially important that we come to a place in our lives where we understand the gift we have which is life.

I finally understand the importance of having that peace with my past. But I must let you know how this peace came about and that was acknowledging and accepting Jesus as my redeemer a place of contentment I'm good with that. Had it not been for the many afflictions that happen in my life I would not be where I am today. I'm in a race to be the best me God does not cancel people He redeems them. He is not good sometimes he's good all the time despite our hardships and what we go through he's there I was delivered from the mouth of people that was my enemy I had to believe and know that there was something much better ahead for me I had to keep believing that it's going to work out like I know it will.

I had to come to a place where I knew I must stand still in what I believe and know because life is full of surprises, twists, and turns that we don't always see coming at us. Hold on because change is coming, and things will work out for the better. For many years, I carried around the heaviness of anger and unforgiveness. Instead of moving past it I chose to stay in that prison of addiction in my own negative emotions. Because I didn't understand how important it was to let go. I remember the day I got hit by the car I was suppose to be left for dead, but they didn't know neither did I that there was a much greater force at work and that it was not going to end the way it happened. In the meantime, I didn't realize that I was showing people what God was like. Because that day He showed up and showed out for me his child. At that time, I wasn't aware of his unfailing love for me because I was deep into my addiction which consisted of drugs, drinking, cigarettes, and homelessness.

Another miracle had been performed that day for me and I won in other words I came out victorious no weapons formed against me proposed that day and Hell lost another because I am free from the abuse of drugs and alcohol. Whatever you are going through and whatever has happened in your past know that your life matters and can be restored. He will bring people into your life on purpose just to get you where he wants you to be at that time. What I thought would take years to accomplish where I am today, the turn around happened suddenly. It's not over until He says it over, you'll finish what you started value your time making every second count in your life. Because time is the currency of life. We live in a physical world we have a supernatural spirit that lives within us. We have access to the supernatural. Always remember the true meaning of life is love.

Hello, my name is *Althea C. Moser Driver*, and this is my story. I hope that it will help and encourage those who are ready to make a difference in the world. After overcoming my battle being addicted to drugs and alcohol which led to many downfalls in my life including homelessness. May It bless and encourage you to know that you are not alone on your journey. I am here to give you the support and strength to know that you can do and be whatever you choose to be in this lifetime. May it give you the peace, joy and happiness that will enable you to move forward with your life, making a mark that cannot and will not be erased?

For many years I dealt with the strong holds of addiction the drugs and alcohol, which lead to homelessness and many other atrocities that came along with it. I am sharing with you the before and aftereffects of what life was like for me as I face so many trouble times. Even in the good days of laughter and fun there were always unexpected dangerous pain staking moments experiencing life in a world of uncertainties good and evil darkness and light. But my world was more consumed with darkness than light at the time I didn't see it that way for over 20 years I had lived a life of insecurity. Not knowing what to expect from day to day, not to mention when you are an addict, your life is already a time bomb waiting to explode, the reason being is because it was what I liked doing. I had convinced myself there was nothing wrong with it. I couldn't see this because I was caught up in my addictive behavior and you are dealing with the battling effects of the mind. Our minds are the controlling force over everything we think and do. That's why it is so important that we make wise decisions.

Unfortunately, when you chose to live a life of addiction such as drugs and alcohol, you are preparing yourselves for the downfall of many harsh and brutal attacks that life has to offer going through the difficulties and challenges that we all face living that lifestyle even unto death. I will never forget how determined I was through everything I had dealt with to continue and not give up or quit. Knowing how important it was to end that part of my life. Because I was already going through hell and the only thing I could do was keep going. I knew that I could not change what had happened because it was my past. But I was determined not to let it discourage me from living the good and abundant life that I was given, and I was supposed to have it's a gift that's been given to each one of us. I have come to understand that after coming out of that way of living I realized how fortunate I am to have a life and know that it's worth living.

Don't allow the distractions and busyness of everyday life to take you off course. Ask yourself what I'm doing that's moving me toward my given destination? Is this my true purpose in life. Or am I wasting time being busy and not really making any progress. One thing that I have recognized and appreciate about life to me is that it's a precious jewel so intimately thought of and the process that it was formed in is truly astonishing. How can one not appreciate it? If you could pick one word to describe the world in which we live today, what would it be? Yet with everything that's happening in our lives we soon forget how important it is to think before we act. If you can see the vision, you can see the impossible.

Chapter 1
There is good in all of us

Loving yourself simply means accepting your strengths and weaknesses, and knowing who you are making a commitment to work on correcting what needs to be done. We were designed by an intelligent being life in the beginning can be very difficult to appease yourself too. And misery is an option you do have a choice in the matter sometimes we choose to be miserable but when we relax everything within you will come forth. Loving yourself paves the way for all you want and need continually keeping the picture in your mind of the goals you are desiring to reach will make a big difference. I've learned that everybody is not going to like me, and I am ok with that when you aim at nothing you can't miss.

When your goals or vague, your achievements will be just as vague. A great story is a show me story. And this is what I want to talk about when I was coming out of my grueling times of being in bondage to drugs and alcohol, I knew within myself that I wanted change. A deep, honest relationship requires time and effort but as human beings we all have physical, mental, and emotional limits that we cannot ignore. People fail because they plan to fail when you don't plan to succeed you are planning to fail. When you make no plans at all you are planning to fail. Failure is just the beginning to start again, this time with better opportunity and not to give up. We must all believe and know that peace is the clearest sign of God's endorsement on anything. His plan is the only one that works.

In writing my story I received positive feedback from family and friends' people that I knew and didn't know I was thankful for all the encouragement and support it came at a time when I really needed it. When graduating from high school, we all went in different directions which was the case with me and so many of my classmates but as the years went by, I had the opportunity to reconnect with some and it was a good thing to meet and see how our lives had changed over the years. I know there were times when disruptive thinking had to come into play if we are going to grow you are going to have to disrupt some things. There is no way to be creative without disruption. And I know there were times when they wondered about me not knowing if I was dead or alive. My story I hope and pray that it brought closure in lots of ways as to how my life was transformed, I learned through it all that every moment we have been given by God is preparatory time. The one thing we must remember in this life is that we are not put here to last forever, and we should try and live our lives to the fullest. Once you come to the realization of this it is a must that we take control. We all have been given the power of choice you exercise this power through your beliefs. Drugs is a sickness and a disease in the human heart it affects the mind, your will and emotions. If Christ is alive then there is hope and I know for show He is alive and well! (Lamentation 3:19) – says "The thought of my suffering and homelessness is bitter beyond words."

Life is a series of problems so don't think that you will pass them by, it's not going to happen. Every time you solve one problem, another one is waiting to take its place. I learned I don't belong everywhere, but I do belong somewhere. The secret to life for me was finding out who I was and what my purpose in this life is even though it can be painful and uncomfortable to share it was important that I own my truths. Addiction can happen to anyone it does not discriminate, it's a progressive disease just like depression or any other sickness. I just didn't wake up one day and say hey I'm going to become an addict. It's a work in progress. I have learned that you must work on yourself every day, always striving to grow and be better than the day before.

I am overwhelmed with gratitude at how wanting to change has made a big difference in my life. Today I am motivated and most of all excited about the new me because I have a purpose for being here dealing with real life issues, I have been given another chance at life. Which is to help others find a way out of their sufferings and to know that there is hope it's never too late to become who you were intended to be. Put the work in and you can overcome and accomplish anything that you want to do and be free from fear and apprehension. He is our bridge over trouble water in the great hindsight of looking back at the destruction I created in my days of using drugs and alcohol which lead to homelessness and so many downfalls I am grateful to say it holds no power over me. Because I have made amends with God who created me, and I am fixed and wholesome.

"Making Peace with My Past" has brought lots of closure in so many different forms to know that finally I have come to a place where I realize that life is a sparkling diamond. And along with that diamond sometimes it causes our thinking to change it gives the ability to bring people together is what makes people great. Keep doing what's right after everything that's happened being here it truly is amazing to me now that this day has come, I am writing Yes, another *(Book)* about my past life of being addicted to drugs and alcohol which lead to homelessness and overcoming the odds of it all. The difference now is that I am making amends with the past which is giving me peace.

The need and want to get what used to make me feel good no longer exists in my life. I don't have the desire to pick up and use it again. It's not even a thought because my life is filled with the fullness of knowing that I have won. Thanking the highest for giving me a mind to want change and disrupt that thinking put me in an element to thrive and grow. Making it possible to see the outcome of it all and how far I have come since my life changing transformation is nothing short of a miracle, I must tell you this change didn't take place over night it was a one day at a time process with focus and determination to stay the course because coming out of that world is truly a battle with the mind. I am thankful that I came to the crossroads of change, which was a very big and bold step for me.

I was determined to continue down that path of knowing there was a much better life than the one I had been used to living. I had consumed that lifestyle for years too many to be exact precious time that was wasted. Time that I didn't realize the value of and how important it is to be a good steward with my time and appreciate each moment making the best of it. There were mountains that I started climbing but never made it to the top because I was too weak for the climb. Always wanting that fix upon coming out not knowing what each day would bring. It was a feeling like none other I knew I had made the right decision to change from that way of living which almost destroyed me.

It was an awakening to the real world of being and addict addicted to the real world of drugs, alcohol, and homelessness. After going through this and experiencing how dangerous it is to live that type of lifestyle especially for a woman, there are consequences for everything you do. I did drugs which caused me to lose everything I had accomplish and worked for except my life. Our lives hold us accountable all the time you are doing drugs you are destroying your body, your life, and your soul. These drugs just suck the life out of you. If I knew then what I know now I would not have ever touched it. I must say that I am grateful for all the love and support that I received from people all over the world. It made me feel special to know that people were supportive in reading about me and what it was like being on drugs and to know I am making a difference in someone's life is remarkable.

Because today I am doing positive things in a much better place and most of all I know who I am. The way we think, and act makes all the difference in who we are and how we live our lives. What does your character say about you? Living in that world brought me to a place where change was a must *"DO or DIE"* those were my two choices at the time which was critical. By overcoming an eradicated mind, you can be clear you can be you. You can remake yourself and your fate your body is something you use it's not who you are I could only pray and ask God to please help me not knowing that he would even answer my prayers. because of the way my life had turned out, but my prayers were answered with a strong willingness to change. To have peace in your life that we are all searching for to give us understanding because you can't go back to yesterday, it's gone yes, I made some mistakes and I regret them in every way, but I cannot undo what's been done. I am not the exception I am an average ordinary woman who chose every day to make decisions some that were not good ones.

Who said I want to drastically change my life? And I was just crazy enough to believe that it doesn't matter the color of my skin or where I come from it doesn't matter religion. It doesn't matter about my background, it doesn't matter my origin, none of that means my future that just the circumstances of where I came from that's not what defines me or my future, I just believe that. Not that it validates. But faith is believing in the unseen anyway. So, I had enough to go like I know I don't have to necessarily see it yet there is so much value in what you learn sometimes the best thing you can do is unlearn some things. Because we have all these forms of information coming to us like books, radio, television, internet, Artificial Intelligence *"Ai"* that we want to learn and be a part of but sometimes our biggest breakthrough is what you unlearn and then you relearn.

Sometimes you must disrupt your soil, take up the dry dirt that's been planted for years, this is what my mother taught me if it not helping you let it go and plant new seeds. Living your everyday life is about realizing I can be reborn to my possibility, living my life is about recognizing that I have brilliance in me. And not being willing to dim my light one more time living my best is what I can do with my life so that it becomes infectious to someone else by being persistent and staying the course never giving up on who I am and where I have come from.

To have something different, everything you touch is impacted by your story. What makes a great story is the willingness to take risks? I made mistakes that I grew from my mistakes cause me to start looking for positivity in myself because I had enough heartache. We sometimes have emotions that we do not have the language for because we cannot relate to the situation at hand. I am so glad I survive because it's the experience in which all our needs are easily met, and our desires spontaneously fulfilled.

Your health is also important because if you are not in good health, you can't become who you are meant to be if you are negative toward yourself. Today I am comfortable in my own skin and most of all I am no longer against myself. I had enough heartache and everything I went through was worth it. Living isn't measured in years it's measured in moments. Remember your failure does not stop your destiny. Abundance is the reward at the end of your life. Literally you will measure the quality of your life by the quality of the relationship you had with others and the things that's going on with you.

You will start looking at relationships at a higher level as you get older to have something more you must do something you have not done yet. I had to say things I didn't want to say do things I didn't want to do or feel like doing to have the life I knew I wanted. There were times that were very different, very challenging, I was living in a very psychotic, dark and evil world. I didn't have a lot of hope or belief in myself, and things were very dismal at some point, I knew I had to turn my life around and know that life had to be better than what I was dealing with at the time all this was going on.

Had not it been for drugs in my life I would have achieved and accomplish so much more to be honest I don't know what was going on in my head. The one thing I do know is that change was desperately needed. Addiction makes you not care that you are wasting your life away I don't care who you are you are not going to function better on drugs, an abundant life starts on the inside and works its way out I needed a savior. Whomever I choose it to be people, or Jesus I had concluded that I needed help and so I chose Jesus. Because learning of his love for me I knew he would never leave me nor forsake me. I've learned that people will let you down. When you lose all hope, and you don't know JESUS there is nothing left to fill the truest expression of yourself as a human being. You want to max out your humanity by using your energy to lift yourself, your family, and the people around you.

Theologian Howard Thurman said it best he said don't ask yourself what the world needs, ask yourself what makes you come alive then go do that because what the world needs is people who have come alive. Amen! It's going to come times in your existence when you may stumble and fall, like we all do, and no doubt you will have questions and you will have doubts about your path. We learn from every mistake what is your calling, when you learn teach, when you get give and that's when your story gets good because God has a purpose for your life.

It's not an easy thing to do making amends with your past when you know what the past was like for you and the downfalls that you faced through it all. Overcoming horrific situations like drugs and alcohol addiction which lead to homelessness and many complications that you experience can be very difficult to do. Getting to that place in life was never expected to be. I felt as though my life had been so badly shattered that making or even seeing peace anywhere in my life was nowhere near me or what I wanted. It was all a dream. Somethings I dreamed I thought would never happen because of my life having been so brutally damaged. From the harsh abuse of the addictions that I was so accustomed to using until I was just a nobody wandering aimlessly through life with no purpose or plans just existing.

We don't always see what the person is going through in the addiction such as myself when I was dealing with my atrocities. There were some that did see my journey and it was a lesson to be learned but not everyone sees what addiction does to one's life when you are experiencing that type of trauma for the most part you see the after effects if you are fortunate to overcome. I must say this is a vicious cycle of life and the nature of it is dangerous to your livelihood. Since overcoming my addiction, I have learned to value, celebrate, and appreciate life. Because everything has an expiration date, we were designed by the creator of the universe and there is a time for everything and one of them is the fact that it doesn't last forever, not in the world we live in today. But we are a spirit that will never die. I love the book of Ecclesiastes where the teacher King Solomon is speaking clearly about his making of everything and how meaningless completely meaningless it is so that we can prepare ourselves for eternity and what's to come. Making the fact that what we see, touch, and feel is temporal and want last forever or we can confidently accept the responsibility he gives us no matter the role because he has promised to be with us always. Matthew – 28:20

Chapter 2
Is a transformed life worth living

YES! A transformed life to me is a life empowered by change, being healed from the abuse of your past to know the controls of yesterday exist no more. A transformed life is living from the inside out a life that has been restored and made whole again. It's nothing like having confidence in yourself knowing that your life has been forever changed into a new and completely changed person. I focus each day to try and live as healthy as possible. I don't let fear take up space in my mind. I'm not saying it doesn't try to come because I am human but knowing that I have the power to take authority and speak over my situation I can rein.

This is what I love about the new me. I know better is coming. After overcoming the addiction my next commitment is to stay focused on the new changes and obligations of having a life of responsibility. Because each day was an eye opener for me knowing I had a responsibility to live the life I had been given and to make wise decisions along the way. Starting over was not easy because things were different from what I was used to dealing with.

Now that I'm back to having a fulfilled secure life again this is where the real test comes in or you ready can you handle your new circumstances of being a responsible person after years of being abuse to drugs, alcohol and homelessness. It's something you must prepare and train yourself for my mind was trying to make me feel the guilt, pain, and agony of the past all over again. To believe that you want make it, you've been gone too long and there is no way you can handle or survive this. Your memory is not as sharp and effective as it used to be you try to remember things but it's hard for you because of the cigarettes, alcohol, and drugs which has damaged your mind.

But that's where my faith and determination came into play because the power of belief was all I needed to hear and know to make my dream come true. I was confident that I was going to turn things around a reality check of the world that awaits me today and forever moving forward to living my best life is to believe in myself. And I must say there have been lots of challenges and changes since coming out of my addiction and into the new and transformed life that I am living today which was a roller coaster where there were lots of insecurities that was surrounded by fear. I could have easily given up but giving up wasn't an option I had too much to live for and doing it is so profoundly indescribable you can't possibly know how things in life are going to turn out until you start living it.

That's when time is about to overtake you. Then it's up to you to start making the right choices if it's not on the right path. You don't realize when you are going through difficulties how precious time is. I know I didn't but when I came out of the storms of addiction, depression, anxiety, and homelessness from the abuse of drugs and alcohol that I had dealt with for years. I began to see break through my life being changed, it's not that I don't have memories of the past, but time let me know I must move on. It's like I said earlier, I came out with a strong willingness to continue to be the overcomer that I have become despite my circumstances. It was my time and there is no time like the present when you are recovering from the pain of drug addiction, insecurity, and mistakes that you have made in life.

There is no way of changing the past, but you can change your way of thinking and make it better. When you are recovering from hurt or past mistakes some people will tell you to forget the past, but the truth is that we need to consider our past, present, and future if we want to build our life in a healthy and balanced way let's consider the present it's true that we can't change the past, but we have been forgiven for it. True we don't know what the future holds for us (1 John – 1:9) says – But if we confess our sins to him, he is faithful and just forgive us our sins and cleanse us from all wickedness. You know ever since I have been writing this book, I have tried to use God as less as possible because I didn't want to sound so righteous or religious as some may think.

But let me tell you this the more I tell you my story the more I see God in every situation, and I cannot and will not leave him out of the equation no matter what the world thinks about my story. He is the reason I am here today to share this with you. I must share the good news of His love and how he delivered me despite my many failed attempts to try and overcome because without him your life is meaningless and hopeless you have nothing to live for. Never forget that Jesus loves us more that we can imagine. He loves you more than he loves himself and he proved it by dying in your place so that you could one day choose to have an internal life with him and the father.

I hope that you understand what I am saying and know that this is real; we are living in a confused and mixed-up world I've learned that happiness depends on circumstance. Now you are happy and when it's gone you are sad because you are not happy it's not happening, I'm getting ready to shift because I can call to my God who has no limits. When I need rest, he can renew my strength I serve a God who will always fight for me we all have a story because we all have a past, and we should praise him for saving us. I am forever grateful being a student of Grace there were things I learned we must do to develop a heart for God. Either sin will keep you from the bible or the bible will keep you from sin. We must desire a hunger for the word, we must develop a hearing for it will give you the peace that surpasses all understanding.

Making peace with my past enabled me to move forward with confidence in myself. Knowing that my past had been forgiven. Forgiveness has taught me a lot if I want to have a future and a successful life, we must know the very essence of forgiving one another. Learning the importance of forgiveness is key in our lives to be honest with yourself and others. There were lots of things I had to overcome that were very difficult. My past was very brutal and the knowledge of how to deal with the pain was not there. I didn't know how to go about handling my situations and circumstances at that time.

I was in a dark and evil place of total despair not knowing what to do when I stated in my book Reborn Unconditional love about the transformation and the peace that came over me, the tears that were unstoppable reminded me of Mary Magdalene, in the bible when she wash the feet of Jesus with her tears because of the love and compassion that she felt in His presence that change was taking place in her life. and I felt that same effect when I had my awakening moment where the tears were unstoppable and the warmth that I felt at the time. I felt his loving arms wrap around me as my head laid on his shoulders the comfort of peace and rest like nothing I had ever felt before. And this was after the loss of my husband that I experienced this moment of relaxation and restoration.

With Him the reassurance was so real and what was happening was so deeply embraced that all I could say or thank was what a moment in time that was for me. If there were a thousand words to share about that moment I would get lost not knowing where to begin I was caught up in His time. Precious time we go through sometimes difficult cycles in our life that we don't always understand. Writing was becoming very painful for me because there was always something jumping out at me. Distractions I call them, which cause me to keep delaying what God had put with in me to do.

When I realized and understood that the pain wasn't going away until I completed my task it became a beautiful process because the understanding of my gifts was developing within me. We were created with a longing to know that we matter. We are also designed to find that fulfillment of that desire I look forward to moving to the next levels of life because I want to be the help and support channel for those that needs to be encouraged or just hear the words, I love you and I am here for you. The one thing I'm learning as I write is that it's an *"Art"* to the way you write to reach those who need to hear the message you are sending that whatever is going on in their lives don't give up, there is hope. Tell yourself I will preserve it like anything else in life we must discover it.

Have you ever wished you could go back and undo past mistakes that you've made or undo the past period. To be honest, I think we all have and there were times when I wish I could do just that some of us lives with a tremendous amount of guilt because of past mistakes we've made I would often time feel the quilt and shame one of my biggest mistakes and this is just one of many that I had made and that was not being there fully in my daughter's life as she was growing up. There have been times when I wished that I could go back and undo the past or as they say turn back the hands of time and because of that I looked on and thought of myself as being a bad parent.

To have closure when you are experiencing adversity in life means a lot today, I don't look, feel, or see myself that way anymore because I have learned what I didn't know and understand that was the true meaning of forgiveness. As a parent I know I didn't always do what I could have or should have because I really didn't know how important parenting was in raising children. My foundation as a child growing up was not a structured one and because of that I understood what I didn't understand then knowing that situations and circumstances were different and the habits I had developed became very destructive. Our lives are full of storms, and they come in different waves regardless of what caused them, there is seldom much we can do to stop them from running their course, all we can do is control how we respond going forward.

Your pass should be a place of rest knowing that you are no longer there, you have moved on with life making peace with being delivered from the chains of addiction that once held you captive. We may not always see and understand the things that happen in our lives but as time permits, we will I didn't know at the time that I was dealing with forces that were more powerful than I could have ever imaging. Yes, drugs, cigarettes and alcohol are destroyers they are strong demonic forces which can change the course of your life instantly.

This is my appreciation to the creator: Father I am forever thankful and grateful for all my challenges and difficulties that I have faced in life thus far knowing now that it was for my own good to go through experiences because they taught me to trust and believe in you giving me strength to overcome making me a much better person to appreciate life and the one who made and created me. I thank you for your love and kindness and most of all your graciousness that is upon me because had it not been for you and the atrocities that I faced I would not be the person I am, nor would I be here today. To God be the glory.

We all have a story to tell because we all have a past of hardship and tumultuous times that we've been through, and it can lead us to sometimes judge people by what we know instead of what they know. We don't have to see everything to see something but what you see then is what you need to see, if we can practice saying what we see, we would do right by others. We were created and designed for emotional, mental, and physical intimacy to share our innermost selves with one another don't forget to give the gift of yourself to someone else, it makes me feel good because I now realize and know that I was born for GREATNESS and such a time as this.

Chapter 3
The trials of Faith and Belief

While being in that addictive state of mind I struggled with demonic forces that were controlling my every thought. Hearing those voices that were telling me to jump I jumped off a very high wall not realizing the wall was higher than I thought, over 12 feet. The results from the fall left me with a crushed and broken right ankle that I cannot begin to describe the pain I felt at the time. All I knew was that I wasn't high from the drug anymore, I was screaming and hollowing for help and the first name I called was Lord help me. It's something how we call on the name of JESUS when we think we are at the point of death are going to die. Because that's exactly what I did and believe me it wasn't funny then because I was in such tremendous pain, and I wanted some relief just being real about it.

There are consequences for our actions and the choices I made was not good ones I was high on drugs confined to a wheelchair for two years while being homeless. I stayed that way until I made a change to seek the help I so desperately needed. Being addicted to drugs is a powerful emotion that can and will damage the mind it fuels inner resentment and bitterness, shuts down communication and break up relationships if left unchecked. It boils over into an explosive rage that hurts not only the intended target but others as well. While we often try to justify our anger seldom can it be classified as right.

After coming out of my addiction and seeking the help I needed. It was where change had begun to take place because I was able to walk again. I was excited beyond words although I had been broken, I thanked God I had feet to walk with. I realized although it was very difficult what was meant to hurt me it was turned around for my good. I began to see that there is still greatness in me. What people say I couldn't do I did it because I was determined. As the years passed, I started having complication with my ankle from my first surgery- so my doctor, Dr. Maduka, made an appointment for me to see Dr. John Louis Ugbo, Orthopedic Surgeon at the Atlanta VA Medical Center, Atlanta, Ga. Surgery #2 on March 10, 2021, at the Atlanta VA Medical Center, I had a second ankle surgery to have the metal rod that was put in place 20 years ago replaced because walking had started becoming difficult for me. And I tell you that the best thing that could have happened was for me to have met Dr. Ugbo, the one who performed my surgery.

There were several attempts when I went to the VA seeking help in trying to see if there was any way possible, I could have this rod removed and every time I was told that there was nothing at the time could be done. Because of the way the ankle was broken due to the fall, it saddens me, but I didn't give up, there were moments when anger, disappointment, and discouragement could have easily taken control, all the signs were there. I felt alone but I knew that I had to keep going, hoping that one day things would change because things could have been a lot worse, I was just thankful for the doctor that was put in place for me to have my surgery.

He showed care and concern, a very professional doctor who took the time to explain to me in detail what to expect leading up to me having this surgery. And to make sure I had outpatient home care after leaving the hospital I was anxious and looking forward to having it done. I knew without a doubt that he truly was a God sent. After having this major surgery, the healing process began. It was one day at a time, but it seemed to heal quicker than I thought it would and miraculously it felt as if the hand of God had touched every fiber of my ankle. It has been three years since my surgery, and I have been walking as if there was never a problem Giving honor to God.

Before I continue, I want to share a very important story about my friend Daryl, who came to my rescue me at a time when I really needed help because I was seeking out which dog shelter would be the best one to leave Bisty, I had to have surgery on my right ankle, and I needed help with her being taken care of while I was away not that I wanted to because she was so use to being at home and with her mom until I knew it was not going to sit well with her. And my heart was torn because I didn't want to leave her there anyway so, one day I was visiting my friends at Greens on Ponce de leon, and I was sharing with them about me having to have surgery and when it was to take place. And in doing so Daryl, who worked there as assistant manager, immediately let me know that he would and wanted to keep Bisty for however long I needed him to. I was so glad and very much at peace because I knew she would be in good hands, and I would not have to worry about her not being taken care of and treated with much love and affection. Darly was someone I had known for many years he was there and saw the comeback of a transformed life. He came through at a time when I needed him the most. Thank you, Daryl, for everything and the special relationship that we have shared. I am glad that I have had the privilege of knowing you over the years and I pray that God will always keep you in His gracious favor love you, friends always Althea and Bisty.

Leading up to the day of my surgery Dr. Ugbo, asked me if I wanted him to save the rod that had been in place for over 20 years. Because it was going to be replaced with two screws, which would make it more flexible for me to walk he wanted me to have it as a souvenir, it had begun to start slipping and making it difficult for me to walk I agreed with that. After having the surgery and going back for my first checkup I was informed by Dr. Ugbo, that he could not save it due to reasons that was best for me he also explain to me why and I was so thankful because had not this happened the way it did with me explaining to my Dr. the problem, I was having with my ankle as time went on thing would have gotten worse as far as me being able to walk. By acting in the manner of time that I did it save me from the pain that was to come Dr. Ugbo discovered as he was performing my surgery that the bone in my ankle was trying to connect with the other bone and because of the metal rod being there it couldn't and so it had started wrapping itself around the rod which would have created a very painful and difficult situation for me being able to continue walking.

It's been three years since my surgery, and I must say that my ankle looks brand new has healed wonderfully there has been no complication this far thank God for his gracious favor. You see he gives us our lives and in so many ways we damage them it's what we do with the gift of life that makes the difference. Here is what I'm learning. Each day I live life is always changing we never know what to expect. But the good news is that the father and his intense love for us never do so hold on to truth we might run into circumstances, but the truth is He never leaves you. You always have His presence he is always listening and speaking I learned that his position and love never to change it good to feed your spirit because discouragement is like cancer it keeps growing and multiplying unless you cut it out then there is "Rest" now this one is huge because we're conditioned to be tough and stand our ground and face our giants.

But here's your fight you need to hold and stay at rest the more I would hear pastor Dollar teach this the more it would begin to sink deeper into my thought process. God is never silent he is always speaking when I went to visit Dr. Ugbo I told him about my book, this was before my surgery my next visit was the day of my surgery, I gave him a copy of my book. He was happy for me and thanked me for sharing my story with him. When I went back after having my surgery, he had read my book and congratulated me on a job well done. I really appreciated the support of encouragement.

Because of his encouraging words along with so many others I am writing book #2 titled "Making Peace with My Peace" I am going to switch gears for just a moment and talk about the challenge that I had with the VA Debt Management Center, which involved me supposedly owing them a debt that I had not made. On April 7, 2021 I received a letter from them letting me know that my compensation indebtedness of $15,491.29 was what I owed the government and that they had automatically put me on a 12 month recoup plan of $1,292.00 I was told since I was receiving VA benefits that they were going to withhold this amount every month from my compensation benefits to apply to the amount they said I owed. And this was to start May 1, 2021, I was clueless as to what was going on at the time a lot to comprehend asking myself how this can be.

When I knew that I had taken care of business concerning my husband death in 2013 but this is where my beliefs and faith in the creator of the universe came into play and to my rescue. When my husband Alton, went home to be with the Lord April, of 2013 I had to make sure that the Department of Veterans Affairs Regional Office knew of his death because he was receiving his monthly pension from the government. So, I made sure that they knew this by presenting them with his paperwork which included his death certificate, medical records, DD214 etc. this information was documented and filed at the VA Regional Office and so I thought I was done with that as I prepared to move forward with filing for spousal benefits and making the adjustment of taking full responsibility of managing my affairs.

This wasn't an easy task at all, I was really at a loss, and I felt alone because he was no longer here, this too was a big mountain that I had to begin climbing and I was not ready for this. My resources had become less than what I was used to having and I didn't have enough to continue taking care of what I had. In my mind I'm thinking and sinking as the pressure of this debt started to become more real, I had to figure out where to go from here the thought of fear has started coming into play and I had begun to panic, becoming fearful of my present situation. After seeking help from the VA Advocate Office, I was told that it was in other words a no-win situation. I had no other choice but to believe and start talking to my God and speaking his promises to me over my circumstances Knowing that he didn't give me a spirit of fear but of love, power, and a sound mind 2 Timothy 1:7 I had to remind myself of what I knew to be true. Because time was what I needed, and they had not given me any lead way to decide or try and get a resolution to this problem that had existed. There was a lot at stake here.

I was not going to let fear take control of my thoughts knowing that I am a child of the king knowing his promises to me are Yes and Amen. Isaiah 54:17 says no weapon formed against me shall prosper and every tongue that revolts against me shall be condemned for this the heritage of the servant of the Lord and your righteousness is of thee. So, these were just a few of his mighty promises that I spoke over my situation and standing firm in faith and belief of knowing that I serve a God who can do the impossible who is creator of heaven and earth. On May 14, 2021, I received a letter from the Dept. of Veteran Affairs Debt Management Center.

Informing me that this letter is confirming that action has been taken to liquidate the indebtedness and there is no need for me to take any further action I did not owe the government and that was a Big (Achievement) for me sometimes dreams do come true when you choose to believe.

Chapter 4
A Place call Home

Before Alton and I received our dream home, we had a small efficiency apartment with one bedroom that I called my little piece of heaven. At that time, it was heaven to me considering where I had come from just to have a place to call home to lay my head after years of being without was a good feeling. Remembering what life was like for me before the big change took place the whole concept that led to homelessness and sleeping wherever I could find. Because of my addiction to drugs and alcohol a lifestyle that I chose to indulge in not realizing the damage that I was doing to myself that cost me everything but my life.

I am blessed and fortunate to say thanks for the gratitude and love that has been showered upon me but oh how I remember that special day when I was given the keys to a place call home, I was thankful that a door had been open bigger than I could have ever image would happen in the way that it did. But upon recognizing that the door was open for me I gladly walked through it with gratitude and a thankful heart. Because I knew it was for me It comes a time in our lives when we must learn how to recognize and follow the voice of God. You must trust and continue moving forward with your new and transformed life despite the obstacles and distractions that will come our way. If you cannot control it, you must release it. What I am saying is you can cast it or carry it there has been so many wonderful dreams that I have had since living in this beautiful place. I've had good dreams, bad dreams, happy dreams, warning dreams, and the list goes on. But most of all my dreams came true and I am living in my dream home, a place I can call home. I was given the right to dream and that's the beauty of it all just because you don't believe it doesn't mean it's not true.

I dream big because that's the mindset I have. Not only do I dream big I think big today my home is designed for a dreamer and a writer. surrounded by beautiful oak and pine trees, with beautiful green grass tucked away like a log cabin underneath the trees and the beautiful woods that surround it. I am once again reminded of the beauty in heaven and knowing that earth is a duplicate copy of heaven. So, my dream home is a duplicate copy of the mansion that awaits me when I get there, can't wait to see it. When I have moments to reflect, I sit out on my patio in the back yard and see the beauty of it all I can't help but thank how blessed I am to be surrounded by such awe-inspiring beauty that the God of this magnificent universe creator of it all has made for us.

It makes you want to keep believing in who you were created to be and most of all the creator himself for making such a wonderful, beautiful world. Moving forward Making Peace with My Past to the covering of a roof over my head meaning I had finally come to a place in life where I was experiencing a place, I could finally call home. After years of being homeless addicted to drugs and alcohol I never thought I would see the beauty of how my life had transformed me having a real place to call home to live in. I didn't foresee any of this in my future because of the way my life had turned out. I had been dealt some devastating blows after years of mental and physical abuse due to addictive habits along the way. I must say that through it all, I could not or did not see any of what I have today in my future to have these things such as friends, family, a beautiful home, cars, and financial income. I must say I am forever grateful. I feel in so many ways that when you cannot draw peace and strength from around you, you must draw from within you. I have been blessed and highly favored. Only I can say this because only I know what I went through and knowing this I give glory, and honor to God who is the head of my life.

I didn't think I would ever be sitting her in this place call home sharing with you my life story and how I overcame the odds of it all had I not drawn from within that inner strength when life doesn't make sense. I don't know what I should do today. I am writing about my place call home not knowing that one day my dream was going to be fulfilled in such an impactful way until the thought of it all is sometimes unbelievable. To share the thoughts of dealing with the pains of addiction knowing that it is a battle within the mind and defeating discouragement at one time or another affects us all. But if our hopes are dashed repeatedly, we could easily sink into depression burden beyond your strength to endure with the results and despair that you will eventually come up against even in this life. We could blame others or even point the finger at God for allowing us to go through the things we do.

God's comfort is available when we submit to our disappointments and set our hope completely on him instead of our unmet expectations. Without challenges, we never learn new skills or gain the strength needed to endure. Romans – 5:3-4 We celebrate in our tribulations knowing that tribulations bring about perseverance and perseverance proves character and character hope. Everyone faces difficulties for some might involve financial challenges or the loss of good health others might know that pain comes from the breakup of family or the death of a loved one the question is not if one of these will happen to us but when. Isaiah – 46:4 says -Rather than spend time worrying we put our faith in God the one who tells us even to your old age I will be the same, and even to your graying years I will carry you. The dream that came to life is like I stated in my first book it was a work in progress.

But because of our mindset and the determination to keep preserving no matter what the circumstances were before us we didn't give up or let them stop us from continuing in the right direction with the dream that was in our hearts. Because we knew this was a gift to the both of us and were happy looking back on my life, I am grateful I had the opportunity to share it with the love of my life. Today I am at peace because I have embraced change remembering how fortunate and bless, I was to have met and shared a part of me with him. I thank you Jesus for being there when I needed you the most and for bringing us together. As the saying goes, I'm a Big Girl now or better yet a very mature and confident woman well on my way handling the responsibilities of life knowing I can. Because we all have been given responsibilities that are set before us, I have learned quite the lesson of homeownership and know that we all must be good stewards of whatever we are entrusted to have in this lifetime.

Appreciating and being thankful for what we have because everything that happens good in our lives always comes from above and I'm glad that Alton, was a part of my life there were many things that were shared with me about taking care of what you are fortunate to have in this life. Here is another important factor. Enjoy and take care of yourself because it's a gift in and of itself. But you must be at a place where you can see, receive, and recognize it. That is why I am so grateful that I stumble upon the need for more growth, it is something that we can benefit from when our lives are not where they should be. "Make the Change" the sooner the better and know that what we do in this life matters for as long as we live. Ask yourself these questions:

1. Are you facing trials? Don't panic, we all respond differently to adversity in our life.

2. How do we make sure our lives are well spent? One of the many ways you can answer this question is by giving your heart to Jesus trusting and believing in him.

I found that to be so true. (Proverbs 3:5-6) tells us to – Trust in the Lord with all thine heart; and lean not unto thine own understanding. (6) in all thy ways acknowledge him and he shall direct thy path.

(John 10:10) says – The thief's purpose is to steal and kill and destroy my purpose is to give them a rich and satisfying life. Be aware of your surroundings and try as best you can to stay focused on what you are doing and where you are going hardships and suffering are challenges, we will face due to the conditions of the world, though trials are painful, understanding our purpose can bring joy and hope. Trials are something allowed for whatever reason to test and refine our faith.

Chapter 5
The importance of Family Forgiveness without limits

I come from a big family after years of being separated from my family. I was glad when the day came that I would see them all again. Thankfully I had been delivered from my demonic addictions and most importantly excited about the change knowing that I was given another chance to see family, I must say it was a joyous moment. Because my life had been changed, saved, and I was given another chance to reunite and be connected with my parents. I was thankful for everything because it was very important that I spend time with them as often and as much as I possibly could.

Forgiveness has no limits, it's one of the most powerful ways we demonstrate love our circumstances can't stop us from being what He has put in us to be. We must come to that place when you know that you must move on with whatever you have to do. Making all the differences not letting the struggles and distractions of everyday life get in your way whether it's family, friend or whatever just know that you must preserve and not give up or quit. Time was of the essence little did I know how important this was until I started seeing and spending more time around them every opportunity that was given. It was all God's doing in my life as why I was able to return home to be with family before he took them home, He knew that time was coming so he was preparing me for THE HOMECOMING AND THE HOMEGOING.

That day was going to come when I would be returning to be with Mom, Dad, my daughter, and siblings but I didn't know that my life would be change the way it is today. He made sure I knew Him, who He was and how much He loved me was important. I must say it was the best thing that could have ever happened to me. The change all, knowing that the change in my life was recognized, not everyone welcomed that change. I embraced it fully knowing that change had taken place, and the gifts were being displayed in my life. I was fortunate that he had saved me from all the evil spiritual warfare that I was surrounded with and brought me back home safely to be with family. It was a big change from the life I was accustomed to living but glad to see everyone, most of all glad to be home again alive, healthy, and well a big difference in the new life compared to the old one never to be a part of again. To see my family brought joy and happiness because there was a part of me left there and I had returned from whence I came but in a different way. I had experienced hardship, mental and physical abuse in a world of destruction that they knew nothing about but in the end, I overcame the odds of it all.

Only God and I knew how grand this occasion was to be returning from where I came to the place I grew up not expecting a grand parade but to once again be with the family I left behind and went out into the world that I knew nothing about to experience and found my place among others in search of who I am. Looking for love in all the wrong places only to be used and abused by the adversary himself, the master of evil and corruption. I have often said I wish I knew then what I know now would have made all the difference in my life even though I wished for that knowledge it was not to be things were supposed to happen just the way it happened because of the way my life was structed and the choices I made.

I realize that everything happens in life for a reason and a purpose I know and believe this is so true upon returning home to see my family. I value just how blessed I was to have a family and a big one on both my dad and mom's side and to know that I wasn't in this world alone and without. There are lots of people in the world that do not have family that wish they did despite what we sometimes go through with them. There are a lot of lonely people in the world who need to know they belong, and they are loved. The loss of love can leave a giant hole and sometimes you think you will never overcome it. We need to value our time with one another in sharing the love that's been put in our hearts for each other.

When you are obedient to what He says your blessings in life will overflow, in other words your cup will run over with so many blessings that you will be able to see the need in so many ways to help others. Now that's good news some families are loving, caring close knit family some families are not some families share the importances of family and some families don't some families stick and stay together through thick and thin some families don't. Love is not a feeling it can produce feelings it is a decision that we have to make on how you are going to treat people. So, you see we all have our ways of showing love even when it's the wrong way and we think it's right. This is where we all must come to a place of understanding that things must change to become stronger as a family. I am thankful for having a mind to know right from wrong and a heart to forgive not everyone can admit the faults of being wrong and that's because we don't have a heart of love that leads to forgiveness and understand the meaning of it.

We only think about self and what we can get hurting people hurt people and in doing so it destroys family and leaves behind the pain, hurt, and sorrow that only God can fulfill. The rejection of family abuse can be devastating because of those controlling forces of evil that wants to tear apart what God has put in place I may not have been taught the real value of family like I know today. But I have come to realize line by line how important it is for family to love and be there for each other whether you were raised to know and do this is no reason for you not being able to share that love after becoming grown adults and experience having your own family and the love of others It makes you want to appreciate your own and where you come from.

Change is always good it's the only way life gets better for everyone who seeks it. There is such a thing as having common sense about life and the way we are to live it, respecting others and treating them the way you want to be treated. And most importantly never forget where you come from, that's not going to change jealousy and envy should have no place in the family between siblings yet sometimes that is the number one problem with a lot of families. It destroys them I have seen it happen to too many or they deal with only certain ones in the family when it comes to communicating on a regular basis as if the rest is not important. That's not the way it should be done nor is it the way to love.

Life is about love, that's why we are given a lifetime to learn it. Life without love is worthless no matter what I say, what I believe, are what I do I'm simple nothing without love. The best use of life is love, love should be your top priority and greatest ambition which should be the most important part because relationships are what life is all about. And we should all have that love coming from each other my family at once upon a time in life was not important to me but after having experience the trauma and pain staking addiction of drugs, alcohol, and homelessness in which I survived It gave me a new perspective and a great appreciation for family.

After being separated for years in bondage to the evils of life kept me from knowing and understanding how important family is. Some time we must experience trauma in life to realize how fortunate we are to have family it's like the saying goes you don't miss it until it's no longer there. Families were created to help and be there for one another. It's important to understand these principles you are not put here to judge one another but to love and be loved. Most importantly understanding that no one is perfect we all have flaws, and they are constantly being repeated because we are human beings, and we should except people for who they are created to be not who you want them to be you didn't make or give them life.

Sometimes we must be reminded of who we are and know that we all need to understand the meaning of humility and not let pride be our downfall. I can assure you it will if your heart and thinking is not in the right place. Don't wait until I'm no longer living to talk about what a good person, I was give me my flowers while I'm living because I want here a thing you are saying about me when I'm gone.

That's why it's so important to encourage people to keep believing in themselves and know that they can do and be whatever they set their minds to.

Our minds are very powerful when in use it is and can be a force to be reckoned with. Then there comes a time in life when we must sometime let go of family and move on with life despite the effort of compromise and how hard we work at having a relationship with each other. I remember hearing Oprah Winfrey in one of the master's classes she said that sometimes you must divorce your family despite how much you love and care for them. Sometimes you have to love people from a distant if you can't have peace within the situation then you must let go and let God, he does a much better job at solving the problem anyway. He's never lost a battle, and He never will just believe in him, and all will be well with you and the family Oh taste and see that the Lord is good. Making Peace with My Past.

Chapter 6
The Story behind the Story

Often, we don't hear the story behind the story, our life is a very important part of us and how we choose to live it makes all the difference in the world. I know from whence I came the life I chose to live was damaging to the mind, body, and soul. There is a place that we must come to and know that this is where the change starts, which is what I chose to do. Because things were not getting better it had become worse and more intense to deal with this is where you draw the line and know that it's time for change. I had been given the ability to take back what was precious to me which was my God given right to be who I was created to be and to help others along the way.

We all must recognize when things change, we must change the situation that has resulted from the poor choices we have made and when we are persistent things will begin to balance themselves out for the good. We must always be prepared for the unexpected because at some point and time in life disappointments will come and they can affect us all. But knowing that there is a higher probability that you can't see from your vintage point in the valley of despair. If you are facing trials know that God is seeking to increase your trust in him, He wants to prove to you that He is faithful to keep his promises there are times when I must remind myself of these same words therefore, He tells us to trust in him because he is our burden barrier. And he will give us rest from the toils of everyday life.

The challenges we face in life are designed to help you grow in your faith, obedience, and spiritual maturity. The things we go through may be painful, but staying true to yourself you will overcome and maintain the victory. The time you spend alone with God in His word will transform your character and strengthen your resolve to stand for truth in an unbelieving world. Therefore, prayer is so important it allows inadequate people to connect with an all-sufficient God he alone knows our needs and can meet them as we depend fully on him since becoming a member of World Changers Church International (WCCI) and graduating from the Bible School there has been understanding and peace that's come from it all. Learning the true meaning of fellowship and how to live a life of excellence is a good thing I have grown in understanding the bible and how Jesus can be an A plus in our lives.

Knowing the differences in what God's word stands for. My learning days at World Changers Church International (WCCI) and World Changers Bible School (WCBS) helped me in more ways than I would have ever imagine. As the songs says, "One touch can change everything." So, true and that's because it brought the best out of me, I was able to share my testimony of how God saved and delivered me from that dark and evil world of addiction. Seeing how he operates in our lives makes all the difference. I've learned how being taught the truth can equip you for bigger and better opportunities of greatness.

I knew this was the brook that I was to drink from because everything came full circle once me and my husband started attending this church, I understood the reason for everything that had taken place in our lives leading up to us becoming world changers. Why it happened that way was because he was preparing us for greater things to come our union with the church and the pastors of it, I must say it was just phenomenal the way things were taking shape. I was so excited about the place he had guided and directed our steps to I knew and understood clearly that this was it for me and Alton. I didn't have a second thought or doubt in my mind about it and once Alton came on board it was a done deal, I mean it was like I had won the lottery.

My understanding of the bible started coming alive from within I could understand what I could not understand when I would read the bible which was something I could not do beforehand. Pastor Dollar is a God-fearing anointed man a vessel that He uses for his glory I don't say this to be saying it I'm saying this because it is true along with truth he teaches with simplicity and understanding. His teachings encourage you, inspire you, speak to your needs to let you know that the choices we make in life determines our destiny, and to help you through the many challenges you will face. That's what made us fall in love with (WCCI) I was getting feed revelation knowledge and understanding on what the word of God really means and how it must be applied to our everyday lives for it to be effective was divine.

You can never learn enough about the Grace of God and how he works in our lives I know this is the place that me and Alton were to fellowship and worship at before his homegoing. I now understand more as to why we were directed to this church for this time maybe for the duration I don't know because my every step has already been ordered and I must stay focus on what I am doing and where I am going knowing there is a purpose in mind to my destiny for me to achieve. I know that knowledge is powerful, and you can never have too much. It's what we need to grow and be able to function and produce in the manner that we are designed to.

I was created for greatness and with His help I will achieve it. My giving is a thank you for taking care of me through the trials of dark and evil times that was once a part of my life. He let me know that I have been gifted with greatness and the superpower of being who I am I know that I was created to be a blessing to many others in sharing my testimony and the love of Jesus that he has given to us all.

When you understand that there is a purpose for your life you begin seeking it knowing that there is something special that awaits you.

The gifts and talents that you have been given are for your benefit we are to walk in wisdom and in a way that our time is used wisely instead of wasting it. In doing so others will notice the change that has taken place the joy and happiness that surrounds us to know that peace has come to your house showing the unbelievers God's graciousness and the opportunity to believe and know that is what learning about grace teaches us. Sometimes we must understand that wisdom is knowing what to do when you don't know what to do keep rehearsing that over and over in your mind until the thought becomes real and manifests itself.

What helped me to benefit from reading the bible was my understanding of grace and that steadfast love grows when you read the bible, we are reminded that His desire is to purify our hearts and cleanse us. The invitation is to come to Him so he can do whatever it is he needs to for you to seek and receive forgiveness. By reading and interpret the bible not just for academic purposes but to solidify your foundational beliefs as well as spiritually in learning more about His will for your life. You'll discover gifts and abilities that you didn't know you had which will enable you to serve and help those around you understand His love for us in a more effect way Jesus suffered and died for us.

It means that as we commit to follow Him, we can repent, start over, and become better learning more about what forgiveness does. We must all stand up for the righteousness of God through faith in what Jesus has come here and done so that we may continue to have the victory that is already ours. So here is what I say to WCCI and WCBS thank you for opening that door of learning for me. It was the start of many good things to come.

Romans – 8:28 says – "And we know that God causes everything to work together for the Good of those who love God and are called according to His purpose for them."

Salvation is not a goal to achieve, it is a gift to be received. Ephesians- 1:3

In this chapter of my life is a breakdown of the before and after which is a sequel to my first book: Preparing me for the heartbreak I would live through, including a life addicted to drugs and alcohol that eventually lead to homelessness and the loss of loved ones. It reminds me to express with thanksgiving and gratitude what God has done and is still doing in my life. On April 4, 2015, I had the honor and privilege of graduating from World Changers Bible

School which was a big accomplishment for me considering everything that I had been through.

During the start of my first month in the bible school I received some devastating news that I was not prepared for it was the last thing I expected to hear. My husband had been diagnosed with stage four live cancer upon hearing this devastating news. It took me some time to digest what I had been told. It was not what we were expecting too here, I could not and did not want to believe what was being told to us. We were making plans to enjoy life because of the positive impact that had taken place. The change was all good and hearing this made it painful to accept. A pain that you feel deep within but can't describe it. I had to let go of the dream and focus my attention on being there for Alton, he was more important to me than what was happening with school because things had changed drastically, and I wasn't prepared for this.

After being told by his doctors that there was nothing else, they could do he was given six months at the most to live. Seeing what he was dealing with at the time was heartbreaking. I really had to bring myself together and be strong for him regardless of the deep pain I was feeling at the time I was all he had.

My husband was strong in his faith and beliefs and showed no fear of dying and it was all because of many obstacles he had overcome in the past. He had come to that place of peace where he made Jesus his Lord and Savior, and we were knowledgeable of his word. I am thankful for Pastor Dollar and the phenomenal teaching of the word that we were being taught because it had made a big difference in both our lives the change was God inspired. One of his favorite scriptures was 2 Corinthians – 5:8 says "We are confident, I say and willing rather to be absent for the body, and to be present with the Lord.

After being told by doctors there was nothing else, they could do we came home from the VA hospital, two weeks later, he went home to be with the Lord and my life was forever changed. It was something I had never experienced before the loss of a spouse this intense and deep wave of emotion had stepped into every fabric of my being hurt and didn't know how I was going to do this without him being there. As time revolved, I evolved. I have overcome many obstacles, and I am grateful but still learning knowing that I have a destiny to full fill. I must not be afraid but stay focused, be determined, hopeful and empowered knowing that this too shall pass.

These are the times when I heard my father say Daughter it's a new day you can make it. On April 4, 2015, I graduated from World Changers Bible School I am thankful for all my accomplishments that I have received. I am thankful for all the blessings He has bestowed upon my life blessings of greatness, strength, and empowerment I am forever humble. Knowing that, without him being a part of me none of this would have been possible.

And yet as I continue to make my way through life discovering who I am and the many gifts and talents that I have within it is truly amazing to know what a masterpiece we are. I want to share with you that we can be and do anything that we put our minds to. It wasn't easy for me to adjust to my new transformed life but having the desire and determination I knew within it could be done. I want to share with you some more achievements that I have accomplished as an Author. I have written and published two books, in the year of 2021, and 2024, Attended the LA Times Book Festival, April 21-23, 2023, promoting my book" Reborn Unconditional Love a Love That Never Fails." Since, I recently finished my second book" Making Peace with My Past." Which is being published as I finished writing this ending chapter of my story. I am a Veteran in which I served in the United States Army and worked with many homeless veterans' men and women reaching out helping those in need civilian women single mothers and the elderly as well in my community letting them know that you do matter. June 22,2024 I am proud and honored to be the recipient to receive my Honorary Doctorate in Humanitarianism being recognized for your outstanding service continuously demonstrating commitment by contributing to your community and around the world by servicing and helping others in their Time of need. I am very humble to be recognized in this manner moving forward. By Letting the world know that we all belong and have a purpose for being here. I know there are many more opportunities and challenges ahead and I look forward to doing my best in whatever comes before me. I know I can do whatever I set out to be in this lifetime because I Believe in myself and the one who created me. Making Peace with My Past.

Chapter 7
I was formed for this

This is my life story sharing his unconditional love, but you know what it's more than that this book is about a part of me that I value and celebrate the life I have been giving knowing that I am well equipped to fulfill my dreams and goals. I may fall in life but that doesn't make me a failure I have every intention of living and having a meaningful life expressing myself in ways that I did not know exist my addiction has brought me to this place and time and yes it was a good thing for me because in the end of it all I was victorious. So, I say that to say this we have a life to fulfill how we chose to live it is our choice in other words it's up to you.

I can't live your life for you I must preserve to go all the way. I can't and will not stop or be deterred because I know there is a purpose for my being here, we must all understand there is a purpose for your existence, know that you are somebody living on this planet call earth and whatever you encounter along the way stay strong because you will overcome. You were formed this way there is greatness ahead and I have work to do I have been given the power to do all things through Christ which strengthen me. Know that you can do and achieve whatever it is in life that you want to achieve by having a "I CAN

DO THIS ATTITUDE" pressing forward not giving up. The bible is a great example of how Jesus told and shared his story with the world two thousand years ago inspiring people to love one another.

This is what helps us to achieve whatever it is we are trying to accomplish. Because when we do that, it makes it a lot easier for us knowing that we have the capacity and the mindset to write our story and share it with others who may need to hear something encouraging.

We only get this opportunity once in our lifetime to display the many gifts and talents that we are all created with to make a difference in the world and someone's life. Knowing that, it could affect them in more ways than you could possibly image. Because at the end of the day our lives still exist and there is a continuance meaning there is more to be achieved or added to the story. - I was formed to believe in God knowing that He has wired my brained with the intelligences of telling the truth. He gave us this grace when He breathed the breath of life into us and in doing so that one touch changed everything when He sent us Jesus.

I have been reborn to be transformed to a new form I can't go back, and I cannot undo what's been done if you don't welcome destruction, you want be able to kick the wall down you want have friends you want know who you are I welcome destruction the plight of my journey wasn't easy, but I made it to know I am who I am. How to say goodbye to your past, let it be a reminder of how far you have come when opportunities present themselves let yourself and others know that you're no longer there and you do have peace of mind within. Even when we run into conflict with other people and are tempted to speak hastily toward the aggressor, we must seal our lips no matter what the situation may be. And I must say that it hasn't always been an easy thing for me to do but today is where my knowing better takes place.

I can remember being under attack by people that I thought really had a heart of understanding, even some of my own family members. After sharing my story about being reborn to unconditional love little did, I know that I was nowhere close, and those feelings lead me to want to react in the form of the old person that I used to be. But instead of temptation I turned to the one I knew could help me and He enabled me to remain calm and response in a different way. I would like to share about the attack that the enemy tried to come at me through my family because this is what they want to perceive of me. Is you being always sayings the same things over and over I'm told, and I wasn't surprised because I knew this was going to happen.

The enemy is always looking for a "Mind" that he can use to attack you and with my life change he is always looking to disrupt my peace when it was all said and done, I felt betrayed and overlooked most of all the hurt. But God already knew this was going to happen he had showed it to me in a dream just in a different setting the very thing that I experience with my siblings. And when it was all said and down, he brought the dream back to me and I felt like a failure because he had given me warning ahead and I did not stay focused.

But this is how we learn he reassures us that despite our failures we are still His children's, and he lets us know that he is covering us so that morning as I was getting ready to do my morning bible study, he took me to the book of Isaiah – 28:9-10 says, "Who does the Lord think we are?" They ask why does he speak to us like this? Are we little children just recently weaned? He tells us everything over and over one line at a time a little here and a little there. The children of Israel were complaining about Jesus and the way He was speaking to them and when He asked Peter repeatedly do you love me, and he answered but Jesus ask him again and again.

What he was showing me was that he went through the same thing and if he was being criticized for repeating himself then I'm no exception to the rule. But to receive that wisdom from Him at a time when I really needed a lift in my spirit made me know that He was there for me. It made me feel like someone that was loved and that I belonged I now realize and except that the old man no longer lives and the new has emerged. Because I was formed this way and I have quite a bit to talk about but on a totally different level. Not saying that in my past they seen me that way but it all stems from the fact of my being that I am who I was created to be knowing that I was formed this way, and we all repeat ourselves over and over every day.

You can start with the News a constant repeat, television commercial and our Pastors must make sure we understand and that is exactly what Jesus did In His days throughout the bible. Because he knew how rebellious and stubborn the people were I've learned that God perfectly understands our situation and he can help us understand what we don't understand. I understand that it's human nature to react quickly and defend ourselves, but we need to deliberately focus our attention on the Lord. So that we can experience the inner peace that he has promised to give when we are faced with these times. John 14:27 says – I am leaving you with a gift peace of mind and heart and the peace I give is a gift the world cannot give so don't be troubled or afraid.

You are enough! I try to always remember words are containers they carry faith or fear, and they produce after there on kind. And so, you move beyond fear of dominating moments in your life by believing in yourself and who you are. For reassurance 2 Timonthy 1:7 –says – For God has not given us the spirit of fear but of love and of power and of a sound mind. That's enough motivation right there he speaks giving us His promises he wants you to know that His promises are yes and amen thank you. You have got to be careful how you pick your friends because we live in a world that's harder today to live in than ever before.

We must speak and constantly remind ourselves using the mind we have been giving telling our body to get in line because you are going to do this whatever it is that must be done know this if something matters to you, we are often willing to do whatever it takes to protect or care for it. But here's the thing whatever the cost we can't just sit back and say well I am going to wait on the Lord because God is not going to do for you that you can do for yourself. This is one way of delighting yourself in the Lord there no such things as a nonvaluable person in the eyes of God I'm crazy enough to believe that he has brought me to this place in life for a tremendous break through by sharing my story with millions so that they may know the true and living God and how much he loves us so be determine to win because you have it in you.

I am a woman, mother, auntie, sister, and an author I know that I have been positioned to finish what has been started in me since my new transformation of change has taken place. He will open doors you did not knock on your incline will sometime be steep and steadfast when you are gifted beyond your situation. It's a place where people walk freely without fear. You grow up being hated that means they say I am crazy, but I am gifted abused in so many ways but still I am gifted so I let the reaction of other people become my reception. I'm often reminded of Joseph story and how he endured much suffering what he had been through, but God can raise you so high that you don't bear the scars of what you've been through. I want to go back to that horrible devastating life I once lived. I will never go back to it! back will have to come to me this is the confidents I have in myself I must stay connected He's my only hope.

Chapter 8
Finding purpose and contentment through it all

There were times when I would be so disheartened that I wondered if believing in God would really help me with what I was being faced with the situation I was in. As a child I was taught the bible the old fashion way the harsh way meaning if you do or don't you will burn in hell so you did the best you could to think, speak, and act in a wise godly manner. If we didn't, we knew what was coming next when your best isn't good enough well you try harder. I would say I know God thinks of me His thoughts about me and you are numerous and wonderous I had been in church all my life up to leaving home and experiencing the world which I knew nothing about.

And in doing so I was faced with a lot of dark days not knowing how the enemy operated in and around my life and the only way to overcome evil with good is to begin to be knowledgeable that you have got to be what you have been designed to be. It's the only way you will know who you are and the person you are supposed to be by living and experiencing the challenges of life. Will suffering ever end? I don't think so. I fell in love with myself again because I know who I am now. There were many times when suffering would become overwhelming but my day-to-day challenges knowing that suffering is a part of life made it easier for me to access.

We overcome these challenges by believing in yourself knowing that you are loved it's not hard when you know how powerful you are we are all in this world together. We have a destination to reach, and I want to be equipped to fulfill my dreams and goals. Life gets messes but what we rely on is what we depend on, being able to share my story in such an important way really made me feel good and to realize that in so many ways it was going to help others. Because of the love that was shown to me so many times knowing that my life is a precious gift to have. The poet John Donne wrote "No man is an island entirely of itself, everyman is a piece of the continent, and every human is a piece of the continent apart of man in other words each of us is an individual we were not meant to be alone.

Neither were we meant to be like each other, we sometimes live in reality even now knowing that should affect the way we think about who belongs in our house and around our kitchen tables, especially when our differences collide. Inspiration is born in life when you have a purpose. It took some time for me to understand this because my lifestyle and the way I chose to live was not beneficial, which were not good choices. Despite the circumstances and the outcome of knowing that change took place I understood the value of life and the purpose of it which was something I needed. One that I am proud of, my life means everything to me realizing how beautiful It is to have one.

As I have said many times, I wouldn't take anything away from the life I once lived although it was not a pleasant one. with lots of pain and suffering unseen events that happened that I did not see coming at the time because I was caught up during it all. Wondering where I go from here in search of that peace of mind if you want peace, you'll never have it until you learn to speak it into your storm and the waves within which we all need and want at some point in life. I am grateful that I stayed strong throughout the difficult times not knowing what to expect because life for me was uncertain, but He has a way of intervening in your situation.

To where you will be able to move forward letting go of the fear and insecurities that we all at some point and time in life will experience even though I still had work to do I live for today and laugh often sharing much love because love is patient, love is kind, it does not boast, it always protects, always trust, always hopes, always preserves, Love Never Fails. This is a quote I love from a very special lady name "Bonnie L. Mohr." This is what I am learning about "Living Life" Life is not a race but indeed a journey to be honest, work hard, be choosey say "Thank you" and "great job" to someone each day. Go to church, take time for prayer. The Lord giveth and the Lord taketh let your handshake mean more than pen and paper love your life and what you've been given, it is not accidental search for your purpose and do it as best you can. Dreaming does matter. It allows you to become what you aspire to be. Laugh often appreciate the little things in life and enjoy them. Some of the best things really are free. Do not worry, less wrinkles are becoming. Forgive, it frees the soul to take time for yourself, plan for longevity, recognize the special people you've been blessed to know live for today, enjoy the moments.

Do not neglect your own spirituality because you are responsible for it. Your character depends on it. HOW MUCH OF MY PAST DO I HAVE TO SHARE? That's a good question that I have asked myself to know that my past is a reminder of just how far I have come. Blessed I am. Today I feel it's important that I share as much as I feel is deemed necessary because life has a way of opening you up to the worlds around you. If my life story can help heal someone else's brokenness then what I have to offer is let it go forth with much gratitude and being livid as what to say to a world filled with hurting and dying people that's in need of love, peace, and happiness.

Sometimes it can be difficult trying to find the right words to say to someone that's in need of hearing something that can aspire them to keep hope alive it's so needed because we all have mountains to climb from the valley of despair, I sometimes wonder how much of my past must I share and not be ashamed any more of the things I went through knowing that today is my past.

As I stand naked before the world sharing my past and how it brought me to a place of making peace within and given the chance once again to move forward in a positive way even though the enemy thought he had won the battle he lost again. I know there are hurting people out there that need to know you are not alone how much of my past I share can make a difference as much as it takes to inspire you to be who you were created to be. Struggles are a part of life, they're a part of our faith and through our struggles age comes and with age comes wisdom and with wisdom comes benefits. You don't need to revise your understanding to accommodate events that are occurring in your life, the misfortunes you sometimes experience are temporary.

They come in for a season, but they pass all pain eventually passes at some point in life only principles are permanent. You are living a progressive life, and it cannot remain the same. Therefore, declare that it must get better and defeat the attempt of the devil to have you believe anything else. When you experience pain and sadness, your memory can appear to be your enemy, because it can replay the past. However, believing that your memory has healed you can go back there without hurt or loss. Which is what I was able to do time and time again. Most losses and failures are not fatal. Looking backward can never be as productive as looking forward it has a much better chance, and it can only come through your letting go of yesterday. Because it's the only way you will be able to see what's in front of you as human beings, your largest battles are always inside your head.

That's the reason your thoughts must become focused. Loneliness is not the absence of affection, but the absence of direction that changes your focus to create a different future from the intolerable past. Then you would know how much of your past you must share if you chose to do so do not exhaust your energy trying to recapture the past focus on the productivity of tomorrow. We were created to experience, and share love my life is worth living and I take nothing away from it because I have a life I must live and I have many great things to accomplish, my time is valuable and most importantly doing what I am capable, created, and gifted to do and be in the lifetime.

Which is something I must achieve because I have the willingness within me to be and do whatever I set my mind to. I can remember looking back on my life when I was drifting aimlessly, missing out on what was being prepared for me, I was not ready for the task at hand. During my years of homelessness and being addicted to drugs and alcohol I learned my lesson through disobedience and the resulting penalty the hard way because of my rebelliousness to change. And in doing so it made things difficult I suffered tremendous consequences it wasn't until the appointed time now that I am able to see the differences and how much easier things would have been if I had the mindset to change then as I have found today. Which is peace during many storms that I overcame I'm truly grateful the choice we sometimes make and the reactions which cause us to act out in different ways are all part of how we live our lives with purpose in mind. I'm on this journey to discover who I already am.

We are all on a journey to discover who we really are. To get there we must believe in ourselves, it's easy to give up and quit what you are believing in. This book, which is my story, is composed of many words and sayings. I pray that my story spreads widely to those in need of preparation to live a life that is meaningful and with purpose. Sometimes in the busyness of life we lose sight of how important it is to be refreshed. We must remember we are somebody and there is power in us to live our passion. But as we've all probably discovered, this is not easy but with our own selfish nature clamors for supremacy, and the world with all its pursuits, pleasures, and temptations encourage us to indulge ourselves. In Making Peace with My Past first, I want to share with you the unimaginable pain and suffering I went through.

Some of the toughest times I ever had to face was dealing with the world of addiction drugs, alcohol, cigarettes, and homelessness that I got caught up in. Not knowing if I would survive when you're hurting it can be hard to see your way forward because suffering has a way of leaving you feeling hopeless. And one of the most effective strategies was the pain and hurt that I was putting myself through, were heart breaking times.

When you are on that road to destruction it leads to more painful exhaustion and heartache. Because of my sufferings it has drawn me deeper in to God's love at the time it didn't matter what it looked like I was determined to stand because I knew that if you don't welcome destruction, you want to be able to kick the walls down you want have friends and you want know who you are. So, I welcome the destruction because I have come to realize that everything that has been done has let me know that God has the final words of my life. The most important issue we must settle in this life is our eternal destiny. I know that without him permitting life there would be no life to experience or learn from. And knowing that he is the All-knowing creator of this world and the world to come had not it been for his will and plans for my life I would not be here. I'm doing good right now if you have doubts about your eternal destiny reading the book of first John will help you settle this issue.

Chapter 9
Survival is the key to Life

Considering everything that I have been through, and survived life isn't perfect, but neither are we I am in a good place, and I am seeing the goodness of being alive and well. I can honestly say this, so I have changed my thinking to know that I am someone destined to do great things. After writing this book about Making Peace with My Past I never knew I would go through the things I went through such as drugs, alcohol and homelessness which are failures, and you will lose everything if you chose to continue living that way. I have been in deep provision to find out who I am while on this journey trying to figure out where I belong since my life transformation from darkness to light but then I heard a voice say good news whatever pain you're facing I'm here to lift you up.

The past things that came into my future it was so surreal being able to see how making peace with my past was getting better because it was all changing for the good. Sometimes trouble can be our transportation to move us forward don't fight your wrongs because they can lead to a better plan that God has for you in other words don't beat yourself up. Without all the wrongs that I went through I would not be in the place that I am at today. I can see now that all these wrongs were necessary for me to be where I'm supposed to be. It may have been a big wrong but there is a big right ahead of me.

We all face setbacks in life, things we don't understand, there were many times I found myself on my knees crying out for help. As I shared my story about the time I came face to face with the enemy, he was lying there looking at me as I lay their asleep underneath that old trailer not even aware of his presence. But today I know since my encounter and the awakening there was a hedge of protection that was surrounding me, a force that was so great and powerful that all he could do was lay there and watch me. Waiting for the appointed time when I would be awakened to discover his presence and see him that old serpent face to face the one who came to kill, steal, and destroy. He could have taken my life while I laid there asleep not knowing what happen. There were many times when I replayed that moment over and over in my mind seeing him lying there atop those all-rusty iron crates looking at me. Not realizing how close to death I was just the thought would send chills all over me.

Talking about blessed and highly favored, I am forever grateful for the hedge of protection that was surrounding me the many circumstances that I faced in life were there to shape me and my thinking. Don't give into fear, it will only hinder your progress, you must take control, you will face some storms, but your ship will come in as long as the situation on the outside doesn't get on the inside. Just know that there are forces in this world that will hold you hostage if you let them. Take back your life by rebuking fear and speaking peace over your past and present. Are you in the storm today? Look at your conversation, your speech, your thoughts and attitude, the good things in life is how do we achieve them? Well, it depends on what you pursue and consider "good."

What does it take to live a life standing strong. Since moving beyond my past and making the best out of life has had it challenges today is Sunday and I am feeling a bit down in spirit and for whatever reason I could not tell you. I guess you could say it's all a part of being human. We all have our days of good, bad, ups and downs, loneliness, and sadness. It's called life and how we choose to deal with these feelings and our emotions. I choose to be happy in life. There will always be trouble but if we are going to be happy, we must live to be happy on purpose despite the opposition.

Today I have the privilege of sharing my story with others, and the world of the past is a dark memory and a thought from time to time nothing about it makes me want to ever go back. For the present is what I live for and focus my attention to knowing that I have come to the place of Making Peace with My Past has enabled me to focus on the present and where I am today with life. I have been fortunate to meet some very inspiring artistic and wonderful people who shared with me the importance of being who you were meant to be. They have helped and encouraged me to say strong and not give up. I want to give a BIG shout out to my friend Ms. Leonor Balderas, Owner of Desperate House Wears Vintage Store, Midtown Atlanta, thank you for a wonderful friendship and the good times you shared with me and my dog Bisty. She had her own personality and a special way of communicating with you by showing her love and you always made us feel welcome when we would come together.

I must tell you that it's been great knowing you as a person and a true friend. Thank you for sharing your time and business with me in promoting my book and helping me get it out there for people to read. And most importantly my book signing made a big impact, and I am grateful for all you have done in making it possible for me to move forward. You gave me the hope, courage, and confidence to continue pursuing my dreams and goals that they may be fulfilled I wish you much happiness and success in your future endeavors moving forward God bless.

To my friend Ms. Toni Gomez, Literary Agent, first and foremost I want to thank God for bringing us together in conservation it's truly been the blessing to have you as a friend. and I want to thank you for everything you have helped me with in promoting my books and the encouraging uplifting of someone that I never met yet, it's like I've known you all my life. You have inspired me to know that there is a purpose for me and that I need to continue pursuing my destiny in full force nonstop to hear the inspiration of encouragement that you have shared with me has given me the drive to know that love can and does go around the world and we should pass it on from one to another with much love. Thank you for being my friend.

To Mr. Wayne Jones, President of Veterans Helping Veterans, I am a veteran and I want to thank you and your team for your commitment and service to helping the many able and disabled veterans that needs your support and service especially those that are less fortunate. I appreciate the opportunity that I have had in sharing my experience and testimony with the overall support and feedback that myself and as a veteran needed, I can say that I am proud to have served my country no matter the cost. Thank you and your team for your service and support that you have shared with me along the way God bless you and these United States of America.

To Dr. Tincie M. Lynch, Prayer Outreach Veterans Ministries It's been a blessing and privilege to have known you over the years, it was through my husband Alton that I learned of you. Thank you, for the strength and support, that I have received from getting to know the women of God that you are which is phenomenal. You have been a big encouragement to me in more ways than you will ever know.

Thank you for helping me in supporting my story I know that God has great things ahead waiting for you and I pray that all will be fulfilled in your lifetime. Thank you and God blessings!

I know there are many obstacles and challenges that await me. The journey is just beginning. I know that life is what we make of it, and we all go through things and in doing so we learn about our true selves. Because life teaches us many lessons, I have learned that over the years there is no greater teacher than experience how well do I not know this because I have been there and learned that some of God greatest work happens in the darkness it's not about proposition, it's about purpose. He sees the best in us when everyone else around you can only see the worst in you, the things that happened when I was living in that world that consumed my identity not ever imaging, I would have the life I am living today.

I am able to say it's a new beginning and I am "Making Peace with My Past" I had to come to that place and time when I recognized that change had to be made. Not that every day was a bed of roses because there were many ups and downs just like everyone else, it's just that I have learned how to deal with living life in this world where any and everything goes. I am learning to choose my friends carefully because people you think or good people later to discover who they really are can be hurtful. Forgiveness is something we must do, and I know that it's not always the easiest thing to do, but when you do it unties and release it's not a feeling or emotions it's doing what is right to have peace within. My inner peace begins from within forgetting the past, living in the present and looking forward to a bigger, better, and brighter future. Because I had to come to grips with myself where I realized I was different and my knowing of self-had begun to heal. I know longer need to fear or be afraid because I have overcome the addictions that once ravage and tormented my life holding me captive, I am confident that Peace with the Past has centered me around making wise decisions.

Using the wisdom and knowledge given to me I can't let the distractions cause me to lose out on where I am going and what I am doing. It's easy to get caught up which has in the past caused me a lot of hurt and pain it's to my advantage that I am not abused, misused, or victimized anymore. Because I know what I had been through and what it was like for me coming out of what seemed like all hope was lost. Today I am still learning that it's important to be wise in choosing your friends. Everyone does not belong in your inner circle when you choose to change the way you live from wrong to right. I must stay grounded on my purpose and know that there is nothing no greater than having a mind it's one of God's greatest gifts we can have as human beings.

I now realize how blessed I am to be able to think for myself because my mind was kept intact when I didn't realize the damage that I was doing to myself. When I choose to use drugs and alcohol to stimulate my mind sometimes to the point of no return not realizing the aftereffects of what was to come. I am thankful that my mind was not destroyed knowing things could have been much more complicated for me. There is a place in my heart that's taken me to a whole new level of understanding. Live beyond your feelings we are all an open book take of the mask of pride, guilt, and shame. Because He looks beyond the mask don't trust your thoughts and feelings put them in God's care, he knows the hurt and pain we go through.

I hope and pray that my story will be a blessing to those who are going through the addictions of drugs, alcohol, and homelessness, that I once suffered. When you are going through problems and difficulties the hurt and pain of everyday life can be excruciating put your trust in Jesus. He can and will fix the problem. I know this because I am growing every day after everything I have been through. I cannot see myself never ever giving up or being a quitter ever again in this life no matter what I'm facing because I realize how valuable and precious life is, it's a gift that cannot be replaced once it's gone. I am glad that my life was changed, and He intervened at the right time for the betterment of who I was created to be.

Chapter 10
Living Strong and Confident

I try to Live confidently and fearlessly knowing that I am not where I use to be and in a much better environment that's the only way to live having been structured being around positive people. I was living a life that was distasteful where there were no nutrients or nourishment for the body. I was at a very low and fatal place where I was not only wasting away but I was becoming a damaged vessel because what I was putting in me at the time was destroying my entire system. Addiction battles are real in our lives we as people can never predict when hard times might come, like fish in a net or birds in a trap, people are caught up by life's lies and adventures.

What's much more real is your victory in life because the battle is temporary, and you have the strength to do whatever needs to be done throughout your day so that victory is assured. I was faced with situations I could not possibly envision yet required little or no imagination because I was presently in the middle of the toughest trials of my life. My addiction to drugs, alcohol, and homelessness my dreams and hope were shattered and there was no peace or joy in going through. I have learned that life is an obstacle course with trouble lurking around every corner and the way you learn is going through and experiencing it yourself. It's not a matter whether storms and trials may come, but when. We don't have to live in fear and anxiety. but you will never know this until you connect with your inner self to find that peace, we all have been searching for.

Be assured that the key to experiencing peace is to believe in yourself and the one who gives life I now know and see just how beautiful life is here to teach us the value and purpose of having such a wonderful gift. Just think how devastating that can be to someone that doesn't realize the life you are living. I am happy that I get the chance to live life in a way to know how important it is to make good of who I have become because I had a mind and wanted change. In doing so it has made a world of difference. The benefits of Making Peace with My Past have made me more aware, and I feel good about where I am and the life changing experience. "How Good is That" to know and see the love of Jesus, always remember your #1 purpose in life is to let God love you and you love him back because His love is unconditional, He loves you on your good days and your bad days.

Love Him with all you got I was once a person that was destined for destruction but there was a change of plan I was restored, revived, refreshed, and given a new lease on life. Know that purpose does not prevent you from having pain, you are going to have difficult times. Broken trees bear fruit I was once broken sometimes our greatest accomplishments will come out of your deepest hurt. Pain can cause you to develop what you never thought was possible. We can't control time and we cannot stop it but if you make time more important than eternity you will lose out on both. Don't lose your focus because distraction began to look like opportunities never stay where you begin, you must move onto greater things.

If you are going after today, you must release yesterday expansion must be your own appointed tract producing a fuller life. And knowing maturity is when my miracles happen more than my mistakes because I have set my anchor in the hope of knowing I can do this. What constitutes a strong life for every one of us is building our life and what's on the inside of you that determines whether you have a strong life. You only know how strong you are when your weaknesses come along with your trials, a strong life is one where you have grown to believe in yourself. Being guided by your beliefs in knowing this is the right thing to do and when you have the right mind set you can never go wrong with eternal peace that's in all of us.

There is power in life, realer than any storm, in those words I was once a bruised soul who crushed the serpent's head because it takes a bruised soul that has been through something to crush the serpent's head and deliverance was my victory. I speak, share, and proclaim the victory that has been given unto me. In through by determination and perseverance when I didn't think It was possible at the time I didn't give up cave in or quit even though my life was at high end stakes this was one time I believed in myself. So don't let the spirit of fear keep you stuck between the storm and the solution get out while you have the chance. Don't let yourself stay stuck in bad situations and do nothing because of what you fear might happen. Remember the word is your security, it's proof of who you are and whose you are.

You can defeat fear by just believing because He's always with us everywhere we go and that is good news, it's the way He designed us to be a part of our lives everywhere we go. Isn't it incredible how He created humor and laughter He can make us laugh and our hearts are filled with joy. He certainly has a good sense of humor. This is what I want people to know when they meet and talk with me on any level. The bottom line is that my life is centered around learning and living a life that is pleasing to the father reason for commitment is because He alone deserves all of me and nothing less, I want to brag on what He has done for me, I feel empowered, secure, and very positive because I gave it my all.

Most of all proud to share this part of my story I know who I am after everything I went through and have come back from the dead of drug abuse to this place in life, I surrender all. I've learned a lot about the truth even when we fall. Making Peace with My Past has created creativity in me and a mind to know that my life is beautiful, even when you are tempted to say something unwholesome or unkind you must stop. When we are hurting, angry or frustrated, it is tempting to let corrupt words come from our mouths and sometimes we do because it is a part of us as human beings. But instead of this way of thinking we should strive to speak only words that uplift and help others is important it's a work in progress.

Before you speak, consider if the words that you are preparing to speak will be edifying or corrupt, do they extend grace to those listening or do they wound with the understanding that everyone is not there yet. Don't get discouraged by what you are going through you couldn't become who you were created to be without the disappointments, without the bad breaks, without the struggles maybe you struggled with addiction for so long that you've lost the desire to be free. Suffering is a test it an opportunity to show that you are not going to get discouraged and give up on your dreams or lose your passion. Don't spend life trying to figure out all the why's of life why people are trying to ruin my reputation, the difficulty is not there to defeat you it's there to promote you.

I have always known since being delivered from my addiction to know that there is purpose for my life and yet it's now greater than anything I could imagine it's more than family, career, ambition, or even my wildest dreams. I know that whatever is planned for my life will be accomplished because that's where it starts within. I once was lost out there with no hope in total darkness and gloom. But it was only in and through commitment and determination that I discovered my origin, my identity, my meaning, purpose, and destiny, every other path led to a dead end. Paying attention to where we are going leads us out into an open and spacious free life. My life is about who I was meant to be because I didn't create myself so there is no way I can tell myself what I was created for only God knows focusing own ourselves will never reveal our life's purpose.

The bible must and will always have the first and last words in life it is God who directs the lives of all of us every life is in His power in which he created everything. Without him life makes no sense, and I don't think any of us would be here now that I no longer deal with the afflictions of drugs, alcohol, and homelessness begin addicted to something that once had crippled my entire being is now a thing of the past. I know longer desire or have that mindset to indulge in that lifestyle what was meant for my destruction turned out for my good.

I remember when he appeared to me on the cross the morning, I was in my bathroom getting ready to start my day. When suddenly my eyes went to the cross that was around my neck it was to my amazement what I saw was unbelievable to me because I had never seen or experienced anything like it. I was looking at the supernatural take place which is something you don't see every day before my very eyes I seen that cross He was hanging own come to life. meaning the blood was flowing from the crown of thorns that was brutally placed on his head to running down his body it was plain and clear but painful to watch.

He caused the cross to become bigger so that I could see that this was very much real. And it really got the attention of me and my husband, it was something to behold all we could do was stare in amazement at what God was doing at the time we didn't understand what it all meant. It took a while before I really understood the true meaning behind what it was, He wanted me to know. The one thing I do understand and know is that I serve a powerful and mighty God who can do anything He wants including the impossible. Letting me know that I was covered under the blood of Jesus my sins have been forgiven and no weapon formed against me will ever prosper. I trust and believe in Him with all my heart and lean not to my own understanding knowing that the God of hope will give me all joy and peace in believing.

Knowing now what I didn't know at the time is that He didn't give me a spirit of fear but of love, power and of a sound mind. It's good to have a sound mind to be able to think and do for yourself is beyond comprehension because I had done drugs for some long. until I didn't know the extent on how much damage I had done to the mind. We only have one life to live, and we should live it to the fullest. Which is what I plan on doing before leaving this world (earth) even though sometimes we miss the mark at some point in life and we make wrong decisions, the first step to a turnaround is to be exposed to all the options. Because without a vision not knowing your purpose the people perish, they will die not on the outside but within because there is no exposure. There are goals we must set and be determined to fulfill them. Don't waste your life and time on the unprofitable things that the world has to offer you without realizing who you are on this planet. There is nothing wrong with starting small but there is something wrong with staying there your power of resistances is gone when you submit like sheep to wolves, they will eat you alive.

Chapter 11
Finding my Way

Living in this human race we will always be learning whether it's beneficial or not that's up to you to discover who you are and your exact purpose for being here. I now know that I was meant to be here causing me to take charge and be able to move forward and live the life that I know is destined for me. There comes a time when things that you are trying to accomplish can be confusing but realize and know that your greater is coming. The driving force is unstoppable it took me some time to adjust to that new way of thinking in bringing together life's most challenging battles that I have experienced throughout my ordeal.

When I was dealing with the afflictions of drugs, alcohol, addictions which led to being homeless and overcoming the odds of everything. I faced head on and went through to being able to share my story in a profound way that it may help others that are lost in a debilitating world of addiction. That feels hopeless to be able to move beyond those moments knowing that it's not over for you, it's only a test that you are going through. What is true for you is what you have observed for yourself knowing what you know is personal and confidential within self. It's a great need to know that we as a people are going to face different storms that will arise in our lives. But we must understand that we cannot fight this battle alone or by ourselves, we need the help of one another to get through what you are faced with.

There is no way one person can have all the answers to life's problems and if you think that you are, I am sorry but I'm here to tell you that you are not wired that way. This is the reason why God created more than just you we simply need to understand that to accomplish what you are going after we need each other's help and support that is what please our Father. When we love one another sharing always work when we work together. In this broken world the list of wrongdoings is endless. All sin is an addiction. Admitting your wrong is one of the first things that we need to do admit that we need His help. The way to overcome the addiction is to have faith in your beliefs when you starve the flesh of wrongdoing you live in victory.

This is to whom you have existences Jeremiah – 1:5 says – I knew you before I formed you in your mother's womb before you were born, I set you apart and appointed you as my prophet to nations.

Psalm – 139:12-14 says – But even in darkness I cannot hide from you to you the night shines as bright as the day darkness and light are the same to you. (13 – You made all the delicate inner parts of my body and knit me together in my mother's womb.) (14 – Thank you for making me so wonderfully complex your workmanship is marvelous how well I know it.) Your body was design by God to restore, repair, and heal itself. We are also thankful for doctors and the knowledge that has been given to them because it does make a difference in the world in which we live today. He says I am your shield no buffet of the world can harm you practice feeling that shield until nothing has the power to spoil your inner peace. What happened on the cross was powerful enough to save everyone that was born into this world. That was the work of God through Christ Jesus. Ephesians – 2:8 – says – For by grace you are saved through faith, and that not of yourselves it is a gift of God.

Chapter 12
Living without Purpose

Living without purpose can be very confusing, not knowing where you are going is your purpose for living life. God told Cain; he would be a restless wonderer on the earth that describes most people today wondering through life without a purpose. We are products of our past. I don't know all the keys to success, but one key failure is to try to please everyone. Being controlled by the opinion of others is a guaranteed way to miss out on your purpose for your life. Knowing your purpose gives meaning to your life we were made to have meaning there is nothing quite as potent as a focus life, one lived on purpose motivates your life because purpose produces passion. Knowing your purpose prepares you for eternity, you were not put on earth to be remembered you were put here to prepare for eternity. It's not one of the easiest things to do, but it is one of the most rewarding. Start believing again, start dreaming again, start making plans for what is in your heart.

1 John 2:27 – says – And this world is fading away along with everything that people crave but anyone who does what pleases God will live forever. For God has planted eternity in the human heart

and this life is not all there is this is where we get it together down here before the real introduction come into play.

Because this life is preparation for the next there is a purpose for our lives here on earth, the most you will live in this life is one hundred and twenty years on earth, I have yet to hear of a human being besides Moses lived 120 years we do have people who are living longer.

The book of Genesis – 6:3 says – His days shall be one hundred and twenty years on the earth. But you will spend forever in eternity. Sir Thomas Brown once said, "Your time here on earth is a small parenthesis in eternity you were made to last forever just not in this earthly body. The bible tells us that "God has planted eternity in the human heart. Meaning we are to know that in our hearts we will, we can and will have eternity with Him if we believe when we were created, He put within us born instincts that longs for immortality because God designed us in his image to live for eternity.

Even though we all die, and death always seems to leave a deep dark hole within we all feel that's unfair and the reason we feel that we should live forever is because God has wired our brains with that desire. We were made to think that way while life on earth offers many choices eternity offers only two Heaven or Hell your relationship to God on earth will determine your relationship to him in eternity. If you believe and trust in God's son Jesus, you will be invited to spend the rest of eternity with him on the other hand if you reject His love, forgiveness, and salvation you will spend eternity apart from God forever. C.S. Lewis said there are two kinds of people: those who say to God "Thou will be done." And those who God says, alright then have it your way? Tragically the sad part about this is many people will have to endure eternity without God because they choose to live without Him here on earth.

When you fully comprehend that there is more to life than just here and now, and you realize that life is just preparation for eternity you will begin to live differently. The closer you live to God the smaller everything else appears when you live considering eternity your valves change. You use your time and money more wisely so many times I shared in conversations about what is it going to be like in eternity with God. and frankly to tell you the truth I can't even begin to wrap this around my own brain accessing the wonder and greatness of heaven. I don't think words have been invented that could possibly describe the experience of eternity.

Though I have heard many testimonies about heaven and experience the invitation of going there is some kind of wonderful however, God has given us glimpses of eternity in his word. One thing that is for sure about heaven is that we won't be lying around on clouds with halos over our heads playing harps God offers you an opportunity beyond your lifetime. The bible says His plans endure forever his purpose last eternally you may feel it's morbid to think about death but it's unhealthy to live in denial of death and not consider what is inevitable.

Only a fool would go through life unprepared for what we all know will eventually happen get ready He's coming back you need to think more about eternity and not less because it's sure to come whether you are ready or not, we cannot stop what's already been spoken by God. If you have a relationship with God through Jesus, you don't need to fear death because it is the door to eternity. It will be the last hour of your time on earth, but it want be your last the bible says this world is not our home for we look forward to our everlasting home in heaven. Yet I am blessed to be here today and to live in the freedom of forgiveness to say that something has taken you it has overcome blame can be away of escape when you feel trapped within.

Never settle for good when God has your best some people have lived so long in a dark world until they accept it as a way of life, and they will miss out on God's best. I am so glad that day came when I had the mindset and thought process to want to change from that lifestyle, I was living that was deter mental to my health and well-being.

You will never know what's inside you if you don't believe in yourself and the one who created you just get to know him and see.

You don't have to live in failure, fear, poverty, addiction, bondage, or anything else the devil tries to trap you with. I am not saying these things are no longer there because they are, but you haven't seen anything yet. He has your best interest at heart choose you because you are you. I've seen what has been given unto me, I've seen what those hands and feet have done for me because I know that He wants the best for me.

Chapter 13
A voluntary choice to Surrender

As I shared my story about addiction and how it impacted my life in my first book "Reborn unconditional Love a Love that Never Fail" I ask God why I never hear His voice like others do. One day I received a letter in the mail, and it was a "Letter from God" I didn't know at the time that He was answering me back but let me share with you the feeling that overcame me when I read that letter, because forgiveness was all over it. I could not believe what I was reading the clarity of it all although I knew God was involved because of what I was reading, and He was letting me know how much he loved me despite my many failed attempts. It was biblically instructed, and my questions answered I knew only He could do that I would pore over every word, savor every line taken it to heart because I knew He had written me that letter through the heart of mankind. He wanted me to know that He is God very much for real and he loves me without a doubt when you are looking for something to manifest you focus on what you are thinking about until it happens. The same with goals, they are things you work for desires are things you hope for, things we pray for to be able to use our mind. Most importantly letting go of revenge the past is not healthy it's hurtful seeing life from God's view point we don't always see things as they are we see them as we are.

One of the best ways to understand people is to ask them "How do you see your life" if your time on earth was all there is to your life, how would you live it. I Would suggest you start living it with all you got full force letting nothing deter or interfere with your peace, joy, and happiness. You could forget all the good and ethical things you have done, and you don't have to worry about any consequences of your actions. Totally forget and indulge in yourself in total despair are self-centeredness because your actions would have no long terms effects or repercussions.

By which so many of us think and believe and this makes all the differences death is not the end of you it's not your termination, but your transition into eternity. So, there are enteral consequences to everything you do on earth. Every act of our lives will strike some type of chord that will vibrate in eternity. There is more to life than just here and now today is just a visible tip of the iceberg, eternity being all the rest you don't see. The way you see your life shapes your life, how you define life determines your destiny, your perspective will influence how you invest your time, spend your money, use your talents, and value your relationships. Because life is a test. It is trustworthy, and life is a temporary assignment, your character is both developed and revealed by a test and all of life is a test. To fulfill the purpose, you have to challenge conventional wisdom and replace it with the biblical metaphors of life.

What is your view of life that hold consciously and unconsciously in your mind? It's your description of how life works and what you expect from it we all have our ways of expressing life's interventions (metaphors) in different ways. Things we like such as a beautiful home, clothes, jewelry, cars, etc., whatever makes you feel good about yourself is how you express it just know that we are always being tested and God constantly watches our responses to people, problems, success, conflicts, and disappointment. I didn't see or understand this until my life was radically transformed from the old life I once lived to the new and transformed life I have today. The new way of thinking in a completely and totally different way is to know that you are always being tested although we don't know the trials, we will go through in our lifetime but know that life on earth is a test.

He will always and continually test us through our character, faith, obedience, love, integrity, and loyalty in this life. I have noticed that I am being tested in so many ways until sometimes I forget I'm in the storm. My faith through trials and storms and by how I handle possession and my love through and for others. When you understand life is a test you realize that nothing is significant in your life, even the smallest things have value for your character development. Because every day is important, and every second is a growth opportunity to learn and deepen your character for development. I Must be careful who I let come into my inner circle because some people are very demonic and everyone that smiles in your face is not always your friend, acceptable, good company to have or be around. Being set free from my addictions letting go of the drugs, alcohol, and homelessness brought me peace of mind and a fulfillment of joy that made me once again realize today that life is a temporary assignment and what we choose to make out of it. In the book of Psalms – 39:4 says – Lord reminds me how brief my times on earth will be. Remind me that my days are numbered, and that my life is fleeing away. (NLT). Psalms – 119:19 says – I am here on earth for just a little while. The bible is full of metaphors that teaches about our brief stay here on earth to make the best use of your life, you must never forget Two Truths: First compared with eternity life is but a vapor extremely brief. Second – Earth is only temporarily you want be here long so don't get attached. Ask God to help you see life on earth as he sees it by being connected to him as a believer and child of the Highest God. So that you may enjoy the short length of time I have left here on earth. In Making Peace with My Past, I have come to the realization that nothing shapes your life more than the commitment you choose. Your commitments can develop you or they can destroy you, but either way they will define you we become whatever we are committed to.

I have come to the forefront of what has happened in my past to recognize that he created and made us to serve and live alongside one another. But that doesn't mean it will be easy nor does it mean we will avoid getting hurt along the way at some point. We're likely to fail each other in which we will because of the world we live in today and speaking from my past hurts. When that happens, we might find it helpful to limit for a time the people we allow into our life and doing so can help us recover from past hurt and pain and find a way forward. But we can't remain in that state forever or a state of conclusion.

Because we are to love and forgive one another, things that we see now are here today and gone tomorrow but the things we cannot see now will last forever. As C.S. Lewis observed, "All that is not eternal is eternally useless." The bible says we fix our eyes not on what is seen but on what is unseen, for what is seen is temporary but what is unseen is eternal. The end of life is not the end in God's eyes Making Peace with My Past was a healing formula that I needed to make my life worth living for in going through the atrocities of living life's painstaking and hurtful times. I wonder if there will come a day when I would have peace and happiness in life again. After everything I had suffered and gone through living in a corrupt dying world to the point of no return how does one overcome, I would often ask myself. But then I found out that the answers were not mankind but in Jesus he uses people to help those who are suffering and in need of Him. Going through those monstrous times I overcame, and peace was once again restored the peace that helped me understand His kind of peace that would take precedence of any and everything that I was dealing with at that time. I am thankful once again for having a mind to want change because that's what it takes to have peace in your life and knowing that you are an overcomer. As I sit here writing my story, I have such PEACE and fulfillment within it's truly amazing how He will supply all our needs making it so much better for me to focus and meditate on my story. The one thing that I hope people will get or take from my story is that this sickness and disease go everywhere. It has no limits or boundaries; it has no feelings or sympathy for you, and it does not discriminate.

Many of us have been in the wilderness of addiction and we have tried unsuccessfully to fight the battle with our own strength the wilderness is a place where God says, I finally have you in a place where I can speak to you. Are you ready to hear what I have to say which was the case with me in so many ways did the God speak to me and even being in that world I knew it was him. because I could feel His presence like none other don't ever be fooled into thinking that you can ever be fully prepared for what lies ahead sometimes God leads you abruptly into the wilderness.

That's his way of letting you know He does speak to the (sinner) unsaved just like He does the save for example there Paul, Moses, David, and many more that were not saved at the time God was speaking to them. If they had been saved life would have been different. Perhaps when things start happens in our lives it's that God has a way of drawing your attention to a call that he has placed on your life. Even the worst sinners God loves you so much that he is willing to take risks on you. He knows that you may serve him or reject him you may say, Lord wherever you lead me I will follow even through the lonely darkest times, or you may decide I can't deal with this, and you want to give up and quit. Know that we all must go through the fire and come out refined like silver and gold; you can't go through life having pleasure and not experience the pain of agony and defeat. Nor can you enjoy only the good times without adversity, there is something about going through dilemmas and cries that bring us to a place where we discover things which we would not have known under other circumstances. I knew within that some of the things I experienced and went through I should have been dead, but I was saved. You don't have to give in, you don't have to give up, and you don't have to quit. He will restore and fulfill those moments of your life when you think you can't take it anymore. It is then that deliverance will come, don't let discouragement deprive you. He's letting you know that you have suffered long enough in the valley of deceit, and he is getting ready to reward you. You must believe and know that because of who He is there is no greater love. I have experienced His love firsthand to know that He is the God of the turnaround and the God of impossibilities he can do the impossible in your life that's why after everything I went through in my life I'm still here.

The way my life was going I didn't see any of what I have today only God knew and did the impossible in my life I couldn't do what was done in a short manner of time. The healing process of everything is incredible because I have come to a place where I realize and recognize that there is peace in the valley a place where I am Making Peace with My Past. Thanks be to the one that loved and cared for me, giving me that special place in my life you must know that He can and will help you. If he said it, then He will do it for the Lord is my shepherd and I shall not want if there are any destructive paths in your life know that He's there to make the crooked roads straight for you just believe in Him. What a relief to learn and know that God can and will carry our burdens and that he will never leave us nor forsake.

Chapter 14
Live Fearless

When we live in fear it will drive us away from our purpose and distract us from knowing and being who we were meant to be. If you want to be successful, then you must go through the challenges of life which are a problem we all have to face. Maybe there are some of you that can handle everything that comes your way. I cannot I didn't always know this until I connected in a relationship to understanding the truth the more the enemy fights you the greater the indication that blessings are coming your way. You must be cognizant of this fact as a believer in Christ Jesus if you do not know this about life you cannot and will not make it. You have got to know that it is because of His gracious favor that's on your life. You are on the verge of a miracle and the devil is fighting you. The reason he is fighting you is because you are getting closer to your deliverances and the closer you get the greater the struggle becomes. Hold on because God is going to give you the victory in every area of your life, lesson that life has taught me to know. That when I am met with obstacles in which I have faced many to see them as an indication of a fresh move of God in my life.

When people ask me about my God I respond with confidence, my shoulders held high and a smile on my face He has enabled me to have the peace in life that surpasses all understanding. Even though there are times when life can hit us with the most unexpected and undesirable circumstances when that happens, we might wonder does God really care about me, does he love me? Enough is enough. Sometimes we are indulging in certain things to fit in is not always for our best interest because we have an appetite for that thing. The image is different from the reality of what is going on in your life some of the things that you're worry about He has already fixed it you just haven't seen it yet.

But in the unseen realm nothing has changed that's why the bible says we walk by faith and not by sight now do your part and stay in faith until its manifest keep believing for your victory. I understand now why he was so desperate to try and destroy me when I was going through my struggles of addiction with drugs, and alcohol. Having no shelter or place to stay he didn't want to see the powerful change that was destined to take place, he couldn't stop it, nor the forces of hell. it was already spoken, and it was going to happen the miracle was already in motion, it was just a matter of time before my life would be changed forever in a way that can never be disrupted. And today some thirty years later my hunger for Jesus is still there something I never want to change or lose sight of because of his love for me I can never repay Him. He's the heartbeat of it all. Everything that has caused me to triumph and knowing that there is a place for me has inspired me to be the best of the best. I owe it all to Him who has forgiven my past and enabled me to move forward with making peace with myself and the world.

Totally life changing I can only imagine one being in that place living free and trusting in his promise to give me a future and hope. Being strong in a world living life one day at a time and to the utmost of my abilities I will be honest with myself, it wasn't always the easiest thing to do. There were and still are things I have to go through dealing with the temptations of everyday life and the insecurities. My fear, failures, and scars are not the struggles I can't deal with what my father did or didn't do, what my mother did or didn't it's all been forgiven and in the past.

Today, good energy feels with love like no other knowing that I have peace within I feel good about me. Thankful to have overcome in so many ways speaking from the heart because I care. There were mountains I had to face that they said could not be moved but trusting in Him protects you from fear he delivers us out of our situations and circumstances. There is always going to be opposition and battles in life at times we don't always know what to do but quitting is not an option.

You are not hopeless, we have hope we need to believe more in ourselves that what we do is going to stand. Because we are powerful human beings My perception and chance of survival in a world that I once lived the drugs, alcohol, and cigarettes. Which led to homelessness and the loss of everything that I was not supposed to lose but to be responsible for taking care of what was given me. Instead of being responsible I chose the wrong path which I had zero chance of survival. If you stumble and fall don't look back, pick yourself up and keep pushing forward keeping your head held high you've got to believe and know there is a reason for everything that happens. Are you facing what seems like an insurmountable obstacle? Or a situation you have no control over facing such things can make us feel weak, helpless, and vulnerable. Remain hopeful despite what you are being faced with because life doesn't always meet our expectations even if our plans are sometimes interrupted. Nevertheless, we can't change our past or the devasting diagnosis involving the circumstances of what has happened which we have no control over. know that in times of discouragement, you have a choice you can continue to focus on your circumstances, or you will work toward a greater future keeping your eyes on the prize. I remember there were many times when I was going through the pains of addiction, I felt all alone and abandoned my mind was confused and obsessed with the drugs and alcohol that I had become addicted to. But at that time, I was so far into the advance stages of drug addiction until I honestly was not aware of the love that God was giving me due to the mindset I had at that time.

Not knowing the danger that I would one day later encounter in life due to my feelings and emotions. Which can lead to an unhealthy, unbalanced lifestyle so whatever happens don't give up on hope or your belief in who you are know that we are put here to serve and enjoy what has been given to us, which is life. Know that because you may be going through tough times you are not forgotten keep believing I often think about those burdens that I once carried around burdens that I didn't have to carry. I chose to do things the hard way you must know that you are not alone love is there waiting for you to recognize and receive it with outstretched hands.

I encourage you to take this opportunity and find that person within you there is so much more than the labels that people have tried to attach to you. If only we could see ourselves as God see's us the love for one another would be overwhelming in our lives a beautiful unique treasured creation. No decision or mistake changes the fact that you matter you have a place where you are to fit in you were design for that purpose whatever it is. Which is enough for me and all that I need to live a secure and fulfilled life as you plan your day, know that distractions are a part of your day. You must be aware of your surroundings and what's going on with you there are good distractions and there is bad distraction you must distinguish between the two you will find meaning and purpose despite what tries to come up against you when nothing makes sense. The chaos in our world is intensifying and so is our work Making Peace with My Past is the results that I see it's been over 25 years and I feel good about myself and the progress I have made thus far. Everyday wasn't always a good or perfect day but I am thankful I had the mind to want to start the process of change.

Which meant forgetting the past and looking forward to what lies ahead, such a big bold step to move forward in bettering my lifestyle. It was very imperative that I do this if I wanted to survive and overcome the chains that once held me hostage to the addictions that plagued my life. It means going to a place where there are no lies about what happened neither or their excuses for yourself because our lives are made up of moments and memories it's like turning the pages of an album remembering those precious times you shared with loved ones, family, and friends. It means finding peace with that failure so you can make something beautiful from it and move forward finding the strength to make peace with your past. For those of you who are seeking to make amends or peace with the past I want to share these words of hope to help you on your journey. "In life, it doesn't matter what happens to you are where you come from, it matters what you do with what happen and what you've been given." Can our histories inspire us instead of hindering us? How letting go of the past prepares us for our future.

We know that we work best when we have a peaceful mind. A place devoid of clutter and noise but sometimes the echoes of our past failures fill our thoughts and crowd out the focus and clarity we need to move forward. If you are going to grow, then you are going to have to disrupt some things. We all have these echoes of past failures, the times we thought we had something great, and it fell apart, the times we did our best and it did not measure up, or the time something unexpected wrecked our plans completely. Our minds use various ways to frame the past, both the good and the bad through internal narratives and filters, we amplify the positive and mute the negative to make us feel better about ourselves.

But for a moment, let's reverse the setting on those knobs to let the negative get a little louder and positive get a little quieter. Now go look hard at the times you came up small or short. Is there a theme? Is there some common thread that connects things together? If there is, take a deep breath and hold on to it do more ideas or memories move with it. Can we learn something more by spending time with something painful so we can grow and step forward? It is hard, but you can. Make peace with that failure and take ownership of it. Why should you do this? That failure is a part of you, the project that failed, the job you lost, the relationship that ended. You thought of it, you made it, you shared it, and it did not work instead of hiding our eyes and heart like we usually do, let's embrace that failure for a change.

There is no way you can plan for the future and dwell in it at the same time. Excuses are tools of the incompetent which build bridges to nowhere. And monuments of nothingness, those who use them seldom amount to anything God always gives enough to give away you have a gift only you can give. Someone has a need only you can meet joy is the journey where the gift and need collide. The journey will break you, but it will also make you in the off balance and shifting culture as you can see building your life on the Rock is the real deal which is a no brainer to stay balanced. You need to think trials and tribulations can be painful for us to go through to my God, I thank you that with every trial I face, I do not have to go through it alone. May you continue helping me to remember that tribulation brings out patience and patience leads to experience and experience results in hope.

Everyone has his or her day and some days last longer than others. Courage is what it takes to stand up and speak, it is also what it takes to sit down and listen. If we open a quarrel between the past and the present, we shall find that we have lost the future. The greatest lesson in life is to know that even fools are right sometimes. Remember the greatest things are simple, and many can be expressed in simple words like freedom, justice, honor, duty, mercy, and hope.

I often think about how precious life is and in doing so it helps me remember don't let me waste my time on meaningless things like I once did in my past. Let me spend my time doing things that matter. I want to stay deeply motivated on my thoughts and to find my place and where I belong.

Chapter 15
Know what you Believe

We all as people have a belief system, whether you realize it or not. whenever you have problems or facing decisions begin your day by reading the word and ask God to help you understand what he is saying by searching the scripture for help in coming up with the answer. He loves communicating with you and He will make himself known I can't begin to tell you how many times this has helped me in my recovery of knowing and believing that He does exist and is there for us if we truly seek him out.

Knowing what the bible says is essential for developing a sound system of beliefs and founded on the truth and wisdom of the Lord. The world will offer you a variety of philosophies, but a faith anchored in the bible is your protection against deception. Anytime we add other philosophies or ideas to God's word or pick and choose which part of the bible to believe, we create our own version of faith based on personal reasoning. Every human being was created by God, but not everyone is a child of God. Prayer lets you speaks to God, meditation let God speak to you both are essential to becoming a friend of God. God wants your life all of it ninety-five percent is not enough.

There are three barriers that blocks our total surrender to God and that is fear, pride, and confusion we don't realize how much God loves us, we want to control our own lives and we misunderstand the meaning of surrender. Surrender is not the best way to live, it's the only way to live, nothing else works. So, tell God exactly how you feel, if it means pouring out your heart to Him and unloading every emotion that you are feeling. In bring my story to its end I want to share this part of my life with you in knowing that the choices and decisions we make in life are what you believe is best. It's just that critical because this is your new beginning. When I joined the military in July of 1974, my plan was to make a career out of it, meaning I was planning on retiring from the Army but instead I was faced with mental and physical issues that caused health problems. I was given an honorable medical discharge not knowing I would be in a totally different war for the next 30 years. My first war was my marriage, one that I was not prepared for a very abusive relationship I did not see any of this coming because I was totally on the blind side of love. A love that was never there. It was all one big mistake I had made because I met someone who I thought really loved me, but it was just the opposite. He was not ready for commitment or the responsibility of marriage, which left my heart broken despite being young at heart and in love with someone I didn't even know. It was painful but the things I didn't understand then being young and inexperienced I do now.

Because life teaches us many valuable lessons it's up to us to learn from them. Then there was my encounter with a war that had excruciating dangerous benefits, no 401K, no security, no retirement, and nothing to look forward to or show for what I had done with my life. Instead, I was in a war of drugs, alcohol and homelessness, a war that was consuming everything that I was created to be wasting away I was no longer in control. I fought with these demonic forces for over 30 years not knowing what each day would bring a war that one day brought me to my knees in need of a savior. I looked up and realized I needed help and that was the day that my life was changed forever, that was the day I had an awakening. I found the peace and stability that I needed to know that I can do this because of my many triumphs and where He has brought me from. Eternity is a life forever with the father let's look forward to seeing one another there.

Hypothetically speaking, if you tend to prove everybody's past lives you will find that there is seldom anybody who has not experienced a painful past. Even though there are times when I am reminded of my past at least in one way or another which is a part of this journey. We all have faced a lot more difficulties to attain the position that we are currently in but what happened in my life can't be denied despite my overcoming many hardships which are now a thing of the past. We need to always try to remain in the present moment and work towards our future and that's possible only when we enter Making Peace with the Past, I am wonderful. I am a possibility waiting to happen, I have forgiven myself and most of all I have been forgiven by God for all the wrongs I have done in life thus far. I know God loves me because He thinks I am wonderful and knowing this has made it so much easier to leave the past in the past and move forward making peace with it. No matter what has happened, I am who I was created to be, I have come to a place where I recognize how important it was for me to change the way I lived and know that there is a much better life ahead that's waiting for me.

The kind of life that I need but to have it I had to change the way I think and in doing so I began to move forward in making peace with my past. Because I have learned to love and appreciate who I am that's the only way I could begin to have peace in my life, in other words I passed the test. Time is no longer being waisted. It is my prayer that this book helps you in understanding that you are special may you be richly bless as you decided to follow Jesus because He wants to give you, His peace. I can tell you with great confidence that your best days are right out in front of you, develop a vision of victory and make it plan.

In my closing Story

I don't want to just exist I want to leave a legacy behind so that people will know that I did something positive with my life. Not just forget about me two weeks after I'm gone, I don't think God created us to take up space down here on earth we were created to do and make something out of our lives. But when bad things happen, we have to accept the mistakes and focus on life, don't give up, we all have to deal with it in our own way. Every experience is precious and that's life, enjoy it and live it to the full because it matters. There were many nights I could not sleep as I would lie down because of the chemicals I had consumed in the drug crack cocaine that I was hooked on.

I would say to myself this is your fate now you have survived as I would lay there outside looking up into the sky at the moon and the stars knowing that I could not continue living like this. My chances of survival were becoming more dire to accept. I would spend years trying to find that place of refuge, but I realize it comes a time when you have to fight for what you know is right. I knew I had that responsibility and owed it to myself. Because our lives are shaped by our habits and the choices we make day after day. Is it possible to be happy? The environment you live in may not permit you to be happy, all the happiness you will find lies in you. Our attitude toward life makes it possible toward living when you stop building your own. You cannot make life you were given life and when you change yourself you change the attitudes around you. Which consists of being happy and becoming well is why one changes because then we learn the real lesson of love. To take from one is the road to disaster but to love one is the road to strength.

What's true for you is what you have seen for yourself if you think that all is lost then every dream has faded. But think again it's all there inside you, you can live again I've learned that if you keep insisting that you don't belong you never will. When I was in my addiction it was people that cared who encouraged me to make that change, I'm living proof that when you do the right thing good things happen. Your expectations set the limit for your life, in order to change your life, you have to change your focus. I was delivered from the addictions that plagued me for over 25 years. I am a champion, it's really amazing when finishing something you have started. Get ready to accept the consciousness for every choice you make. You may sometimes seem distant but the funny thing about change is when nothing changes. It all starts with thinking when your life starts changing you are going to let go of something and take hold of something. I have one person larger than life imagination because I am a visionary when peace like a wave has tended my sorrow my soul shall stay anchored. Writing my life story after going through the thing I did is not the easiest thing to do. When it comes to stability everything depends on the supporting structure taking a risk and know that God has put something special on the inside of us all. We need to see and know who we could become but it all starts with our thinking. Know this: your creator loves you and invites you to sit at His table in this life and the life to come.

John 16:33 – says – I say these things unto you that in me you may have peace, in the world you will have tribulations but be of good cheer for I have overcome the world.

Dedication

In loving memory of Bisty,

In the conclusion of my story. I want to share with you something that was very near and dear to my heart the death of my dog (Bisty) I cannot begin to tell you how all this has impacted me. I could only ask that God grant me the serenity to accept the things I cannot change the courage to change things I can and wisdom to know the difference.

On Monday, March 11, 2024, at 5:30pm (Bisty) whom me and husband adopted when she was 2 months old passed away, she was fourteen at the time this took place. Which left me shaking to my core with the way everything happened. I could not believe that I would not be coming back home with my baby after taking her to the vet to be checked out for what was going on with her at that time. And yet it didn't take long for everything to play out the fact that the organs in her body were shutting down and watching her lying there left me devastated and heartbroken, not to mention the tears that were streaming down my face.

Because I wanted to help her, and I couldn't, I was in total shock and disbelief. I had never seen my baby in this type of situation and to be told there was nothing else they could do was heartbreaking. I had to make the decision to have her put down because there was nothing else that could be done. And as for me and the well-being of my Bisty I thought I was on top of her health but in the end, I found out differently. I cannot begin to tell you at this moment how painful this sudden death has impacted my life because it was something that I did not see coming at the time. I am learning that you can never be prepared for the unexpected, it has really affected me in ways that I never knew it could.

But I must say I am thankful for the 14 wonderful years that God gave us together what a precious gift to have and behold. Because every day was a blessing filled with love and laughter. We weathered the highs and lows together, creating countless memories that I will forever hold dear to my heart. We had our good days and not so good days but most of all there were a lot of good times and memories that I will always remember cherishing the moments of watching her grow up. I remember the first time I laid eyes on her. I knew she was the one she was 2 months old when we brought her home and watching her transform into the lady that she became was amazing to see. And to experience the love that they have for you is unconditional and unbelievable. I am so grateful that I had the opportunity and the chance to be her mother and to have her in my life.

Words cannot express how happy I am that I got to be part of her life. The bond that we developed between each other was unbreakable. It was meant for her to be a part of me and my husband's life because she made a big difference in our lives, she was so sweet and had her own personality. I must say there was a lot of lesson that I learned from her being an animal species they are very intelligent creatures.

Now I understand the bible when it says everything that God made it was good and my Bitsy was a beautiful, brilliant, and smart dog with a mind of her own. And I think we can all learn something from the animal kingdom if were open to receiving them as creatures of nature that God put here for us to have and enjoy. I can't express enough how glad I am that she was a part of my life and to know that heaven awaits her presence because she's home now and I know that I will see her again until then. Thank you, Bitsy, for being my baby girl I love you and will always remember the good times that we shared together love always, your mom Althea Driver.

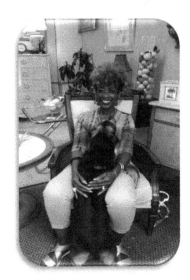

Printed in the USA
CPSIA information can be obtained
at www.ICGtesting.com
CBHW071200260924
14886CB00001B/5